AF478082

VIRTUOUS CITIZENS

VIRTUOUS CITIZENS

★ ★ ★

Counterpublics *and* Sociopolitical Agency *in* Transatlantic Literature

KENDALL McCLELLAN

THE UNIVERSITY OF ALABAMA PRESS
Tuscaloosa

The University of Alabama Press
Tuscaloosa, Alabama 35487-0380
uapress.ua.edu

Inquiries about reproducing material from this work should be addressed to the University of Alabama Press.

Typeface: Janson

Cover image: *Ye May Session of Ye Woman's Rights Convention—Ye Orator of Ye Day Denouncing Ye Lords of Creation*, wood engraving, *Harper's Weekly*, June 11, 1859; Library of Congress, Prints and Photographs Division

Cover design: Lori Lynch

Cataloging-in-Publication data is available from the Library of Congress.
ISBN: 978-0-8173-2081-2
E-ISBN: 978-0-8173-9337-3

Contents

Acknowledgments

Thank you to Daniel Waterman and the team at the University of Alabama Press for providing invaluable guidance, and to the professors who have encouraged and inspired me: at UCSD, Stephanie Jed and Kathryn Shevelow; at Cal Poly San Luis Obispo, Linda Halisky, Carol MacCurdy, and Kathryn Rummell; and at Binghamton University, Juliet Shields, Nancy Henry, Praseeda Gopinath, Leslie Heywood, and John Havard, who generously provided feedback on early drafts of this book. Thanks also to my graduate student cohort, who made life as a struggling student not just livable but vibrant, with special recognition of Kimberly Vose and Sanghee Lee for their unwavering encouragement. This project has been long in the works, and as the years have passed friends and family have rooted for me and cheered the intermittent goal-meeting so pivotal to morale. In particular, thank you to my mom, Karen, and sister, Paige; to the McClellan family in San Diego for providing me with a wonderful writing retreat; and to Brian Rozendal for his editorial assistance and sustained belief in the value of this project.

More than anyone else, the force behind this book is my father, Chuck McClellan, who passed away in 2010. He provided an aspirational blueprint for virtuous citizenship that continues to shape my scholarship and life. There were big publicly visible acts, including forty-five years volunteering with the Boys and Girls Club on a local and national level, but his level of commitment to community was equally evident in small consistencies: every two months Dad's calendar reminded him it was time to give blood, and off he went to the Red Cross (they recommend waiting at least eight weeks between donations). It was a simple and obvious choice to donate as often as health allowed because being a good community member was central to his happiness. Following several postcollege jobs, I decided to return to school for my PhD. When I told my dad, it was not the research or advanced degree that most excited him; it was the fact that teaching would offer me the same satisfaction he felt from a lifetime dedicated to public service. I know he would be thrilled that this project, which began as his cancer took hold, has found its way to print.

VIRTUOUS CITIZENS

Introduction

In *Virtuous Citizens* I bring together two critical stories in literary scholarship that when interrogated in tandem shed light on the shifting landscape of civic identity before and after the American Revolution. The first plot line begins, theoretically speaking, with *The Structural Transformation of the Public Sphere*. Jürgen Habermas's work about the rise of a bourgeois public sphere in the eighteenth century has been expanded in important ways by many scholars over the years. I delve into those revisions while offering my own. The second story is one of civic virtue. Philosophers, scholars, and average citizens have written on this topic since time immemorial. For my analysis the critical touchstone is J. G. A. Pocock's *Machiavellian Moment*.

Like Habermas's work, Pocock's book has become a touchstone in scholarly analysis of civic life. Shelley Burtt, a Pocock revisionist, points out that the term "civic virtue" as applied to eighteenth-century political thought is an anachronism. Augustan writers "spoke of public virtue, private virtue, public spirit, politick virtues, patriotism, but not of civic virtue nor even of political virtue."[1] Burtt defends the use of the phrase: while anachronistic, it accurately reflects a field of inquiry in eighteenth-century sociopolitical literature. I continue this anachronistic tradition and also highlight Burtt's repetition of the terms *public* and *private*. It is here that Habermas and Pocock most powerfully collide. Their work has inspired scholarly interrogation of the relationship between private and public subjectivities, and the political ramifications of available outlets for civic engagement. It was not solely philosophers nor politicians who mulled over these issues at the turn of the nineteenth century; the changing landscape of civic life inspired considerable popular literature as well—poetry, fiction, and journalism.

In *Virtuous Citizens* I uncover a fundamental transformation in conceptions of civic identity that occurred over the course of the eighteenth and nineteenth centuries. Literature of this period exposes an emotional investment in questions of civic selfhood born out of concern for national stability and power, which were considered products of economic strength and the nation's moral fiber. The eighteenth-century rise of the bourgeois public sphere, and even more significantly the contemporaneous appearance of what Nancy Fraser calls *counterpublics*, deeply influenced not only how politicians and philosophers understood the relationship between citizens, disenfranchised subjects, and the state but also how members of the polity understood themselves.[2] When eighteenth-century British female poets applied their moral authority within the domestic sphere to state affairs, they laid claim to a public identity and formed a powerfully visible counterpublic: a community exchanging ideas outside or against the dominant public sphere, populated by male members of the expanding middle class.

As Nancy Fraser points out, Habermas's initial theorization of the modern public sphere contained underlying assumptions that deserve interrogation and continuing critical engagement.[3] Fraser's purpose was to push for a better understanding of the public sphere beyond its existence in the bourgeoisie, part of a broad effort by feminist theorists and literary critics who have explored separate-sphere ideology in nineteenth-century American literature.[4] Habermas left the door open for this form of expansion by noting that "female readers as well as apprentices and servants often took a more active part in the literary public sphere than the owners of private property and family heads themselves."[5] Ultimately, however, Habermas argues that bourgeois public-sphere membership required both participation in public debate, shaped partially by the growth of this expanded literary sphere, and property ownership—a formulation that reflects John Locke's influence on eighteenth-century conceptions of liberal citizenship. Locke's *Two Treatises of Government* made it clear there were two requirements for moral autonomy and civic participation: the capacity for reason and property ownership.[6] Liberalism became ideologically central to notions of citizenship in England during this time.

My reevaluation of the public sphere was influenced significantly by Nancy Fraser and Michael Warner, with a particular debt to Warner's *Publics and Counterpublics*.[7] He demonstrates that *private* and *public* gained discursive significance within the liberal tradition, becoming prominent themes in political and literary texts over the course of the eighteenth century. Warner, along with Anne Phillips, Lauren Berlant, and Katharine Henry, explores a mode of complicating public-sphere scholarship that animates *Virtuous Citizens*.[8] *Bracketing*, a notion that can be traced to Athenian political philosophy (Aristotle in particular), is the assumption that "to be properly public required that one rise above, or set aside, one's private interests and expressive nature."[9] Warner points out that Habermas's valorization of the rational-critical debate elides the private and affective components of public-sphere life. This omission is intertwined with the issue of hierarchy Warner describes: rather than complementary spheres, public life is often presented as superior to the domestic and is concurrently inaccessible to some citizens. These hierarchies are distinctly gendered and racialized in literature, with emotion, limited subjectivity, and privacy consistently attributed to women and minorities. Ultimately, bracketing as a political stance serves the interests of those already in power whose subjectivities are more readily rendered invisible because of their representative dominance in political and public spaces. In a discussion of Reagan-era identity politics, Lauren Berlant argues that conservative resentment arises when those in power are asked to acknowledge that they also "have identities." She goes on to show that "one response is to desire that the nation recommit itself to the liberal promise of a conflict-free and integrated world."[10] In *Virtuous Citizens* I demonstrate that during the eighteenth and nineteenth centuries, political subalterns continually challenged these aspects of liberal ideology, asserting their right to a public-sphere role through direct reference to private identities and in language that represents national belonging as fundamentally affective.

Pocock's work on civic virtue, like Habermas's, lacks sustained analysis of how citizens who existed outside the dominant bourgeois class and classical republican narrative of citizenship experienced cultural change. The core claim of Pocock's opus, *The Machiavellian Moment*, is that the onset of a credit economy in eighteenth-century Britain spelled the death of subjective stability and therefore of classical republican virtue. This thesis is based on an analysis of reigning liberal beliefs regarding autonomy. For Pocock, when the credit economy became more central to the privatized marketplace defining bourgeois life, the Augustan belief that property ownership made civic virtue possible fell apart. Pocock does not explore how this shift impacted the civic self-conception of political subalterns who had always lived without access to property ownership and without other identities (religious, gender, or racial) considered necessary for full membership in the political and public spheres. In *Engendering Democracy*, Anne Phillips argues that although the property requirement "eroded in the nineteenth century," women were still seen as nonpersons whose husbands would represent their public interests.[11] I demonstrate that although legally this restriction was evident, the disappearing relevance of property in conceptions of civic identity created a flexibility in the discourse of civic virtue that allowed women and other political subalterns to claim a political role through public-sphere discourse communities.

The animus of *Virtuous Citizens* (aligning it with works by Warner, Berlant, and Phillips) is the conviction that sociocultural analysis that ignores the way marginalized communities engaged in the political public sphere presents a myopic view of modern civic life. This myopia is worth challenging. The public sphere was always a contested space, and sociocultural changes that impacted this space enabled the expansion of civic identity. While a number of the female writers I discuss explicitly supported the gender divide that rendered their own sex "private," their participation in political debate challenged limitations on public sphere participation. To consider their imbrication in contemporary gender ideology as limited ignores the power that comes from bending rather than breaking a discourse. Lauren Berlant eloquently argues that "to love conventionality is not only to love something that constrains someone or some condition of possibility: it is another way of talking about negotiating belonging to a world. To love a thing is not only to embrace its most banal iconic forms, but to work those forms so that individuals and populations can breathe and thrive in them or in proximity to them.

The convention is not only a mere placeholder for what could be richer in an underdeveloped social imaginary, but it is also sometimes a profound placeholder that provides an affective confirmation of the idea of a shared confirming imaginary in advance of inhabiting a material world in which that feeling can actually be lived."[12] In *Virtuous Citizens* I trace this movement within the discourse of civic identity, showing the extent to which classical notions of republican virtue were adopted and remolded to create a more inclusive social imaginary. By adapting the language of self-sacrifice, abolitionists in eighteenth-century England and nineteenth-century America promoted protest against state injustice as a mode for building moral capital.[13] That opened the field of public-sphere activism to those who wanted to challenge strictures on political involvement without abandoning the identities presumably rendering their participation impossible or at least undesirable. In so doing, they rejected the notion that private and public life should exist separately and offered a new vision of civic belonging for citizens, then and now.

#Me Too: The Role of Counterpublics, a Contemporary Example

While I focus primarily on mapping the rise of counterpublics, my analysis was impacted by reflection on the role currently played by these communities, including an experience that shaped my view of how the public sphere mediates our private and political lives. Living in New York City at the age of twenty-two, I quickly learned to monitor public spaces knowing that as a woman I experienced a specific type of vulnerability within them. One night on the subway back to Queens, a man crouching down against the doors ran his thumbnail lightly along my thigh. This violation was relatively tame compared to a friend's subway experience: she was punched in the stomach during rush hour by a man who quickly disappeared into the crowd. We shared these stories with one another privately, accepting such experiences as inevitable. A year and a half after my subway experience I realized no space was safe. Twice in one month I woke up in my Hoboken apartment to find a man watching me sleep. What avenues did I have for recourse? Was this a private problem to be managed quietly. Or should I turn it over to the authorities? On the subway I said nothing. I was confused, even embarrassed. I looked silently at my harasser as he exited the subway. When a man entered our apartment, though, my roommate and I called the police. They found our story unremarkable and offered no recourse. We were told to double-check our locks at night and always use the deadbolt.

When the official sphere of politics and law provide an unsatisfying response to social problems, counterpublics arise to encourage speech and action in spaces neither officially state-sanctioned nor solely private. Experiences like mine and much worse provide this kind of impetus. Nearly twenty years after I learned there was seldom state-sanctioned recourse for violations such as what happened in Hoboken, my Facebook feed was a stream of #MeToo. Tarana Burke introduced the hashtag in 2006 to combat the stigma that keeps many women from discussing sexual violence and harassment. Burke told CNN she was motivated to create the #MeToo hashtag after listening to a child at her work describe being abused and feeling unable in that moment to either hear the full story or share her own. According to Burke, "On one side, it's a bold declarative statement that 'I'm not ashamed' and 'I'm not alone.' On the other side, it's a statement from survivor to survivor that says 'I see you, I hear you, I understand you and I'm here for you or I get it." As of October 2017, as many as 45 percent of Facebook's 214 million US users had at least one friend who had posted #MeToo, exemplifying what Richard Blaug calls a "democratic breakout," a moment when oppression becomes visible and formerly passive citizens are politicized.[14] It also demonstrates the power of counterpublics: When a community of like-minded citizens share your concerns, stigma diminishes and people are emboldened to speak.

The Me Too movement highlights the public sphere's capacity to bridge the complex and complementary relationship between private and political. The second-wave feminist mantra, "the personal is political," made this imbrication a matter of widespread discussion. Movements like Me Too are important reminders in the face of continued resistance to systemic change. Women asked why they should come forward with accusations that could lead to public shaming, character assassination, and damage to their careers when in all likelihood the attacker would receive little more than a legal slap on the wrist. The 2016 Brock Turner case—in which witness testimony and an emotionally moving statement from the victim were not enough to result in significant punishment for a man caught raping an unconscious woman behind a dumpster—captured these frustrations and helped fuel the fire needed to coalesce this now visible counterpublic. Fraser argued that one result of subaltern counterpublics, which rise as a response to the limitations and exclusions of the dominant public, is to "help expand discursive space." Tarana Burke and the women who amplified her message achieved this goal. In December 2017 *Time* magazine, neither a fringe nor countercultural news organization, named the Me Too movement participants "Person of the Year," aptly identifying them as "the silence breakers." Women and men who actively participate in the movement have the potential to be "transformed from being 'docile bodies' into 'public selves.' . . . They learn to talk *back to the state*."[15] The public sphere becomes a space for both experiencing and transforming democratic subjectivity, civic life, and eventually the official sphere of law and politics. The Me Too movement's impact has relied largely on the capacity of a widespread public community to demand justice. Very public figures, held accountable in the press and by activists, have lost their reputations and often their jobs. On March 11, 2020, the movement's impact manifested itself in the punishment meted out to Harvey Weinstein: twenty-three years in prison.

Because the Me Too movement is still relatively young, it is impossible to concretely assert its impact on political life or the way gender relations are privately felt. However, the marriage-equality movement provides contemporary evidence of a counterpublic's effect on privately experienced identity, public-sphere life, and political rights. Since the Supreme Court ruling that found state bans against same-sex marriage unconstitutional, suicide rates have decreased 7 percent among LGBTQ youth.[16] Researchers found a direct correlation between legal acceptance of same-sex marriage and decrease in suicides. Years before the Defense of Marriage Act, Judith Butler wrote, "It turns out that changing the institutions by which humanly viable choice is established and maintained is a prerequisite for the exercise of self-determination. In this sense, individual agency is bound up with social critique and social transformation. One only determines 'one's own' sense of gender to the extent that social norms exist that support and enable that act of claiming gender for oneself. One is dependent on this 'outside' to lay claim to what is one's own."[17] When same-sex marriage was decriminalized, the many people who wanted to marry same-sex partners were also decriminalized. When counterpublics arise that draw attention to exclusions of selfhood in the political realm and the dominant public sphere, they have the capacity to alter the political landscape and how individuals experience their private lives. Laying claim to one's selfhood in public, first as part of a counterpublic, eventually as part of a reshaped and politically altered general public, reflexively changes the experience of private selfhood.

Methodology

Markman Ellis argues that genre matters because it "affects not only how something is said, but also what is said, and to whom." My archival choices were based less on genre than on the way specific essays, poetry, and novels unpack issues, offering divergent views of republican virtue and the relationship between private and political life. The book is framed by a discussion of abolitionist authors who contemplate the personal and social impact of chattel slavery and share a deep investment in questions of greed and virtue, private and national morality. Chapters 2 and 3 deal with romantic visions of the United States that imagine in its founding the possibility of escaping Old World corruption and writing civic virtue into the national imaginary. In regards to genre, my thematically based choices emerge from a scholarly perspective that recognizes substantial value in analysis of popular literature. In *The Anarchy of Empire* Amy Kaplan argues that genres often seen as oppositional are in fact connected in important and revelatory ways. As evidence she unpacks the dynamic relationship between political and popular discourse. Kaplan proves the efficacy of combining inquiry into works considered representative of the culture due to their firm position within the canon, with analysis of popular genres that captured the public imagination and disseminated political feeling to a broader audience. I have honored that tenet in my own scholarship, following in the footsteps of Kaplan and of Jane Tompkins, who argued that for scholars to appreciate literature that had been ignored by critics due to "unoriginality," they needed to read through a new lens. The tropes of sentimental literature are what give it political force. Authors like Harriet Beecher Stowe, Tompkins asserts, tapped into shared cultural values and easily processed imagery in order to impact their audience. Because I unravel dominant tropes in the discursive construction of national identity and negotiations of the private/public/civic realms, every chapter features at least one work that would have been read by a broad audience, from the poetry of Hannah More and Anna Letitia Barbauld to the best-selling novel of the nineteenth century, *Uncle Tom's Cabin*. As Tompkins pointed out, what is often most meaningful is their affiliations, the repetition of anxieties and patterns in ameliorative responses, which expose their meaning as cultural artifacts.[18] At the same time, I also use less canonical academic and didactic books, including the work of moral philosophers like Adam Smith, David Hume, and Harriet Martineau, to contextualize these narratives and show how actively engaged popular authors were with contemporary sociopolitical conversations.

Equally important to my methodology is the growth of transatlantic studies. Two essay collections titled *Transatlantic Literary Studies* were published between 2007 and 2012, reflecting a widespread movement and promoting an active level of disciplinary self-assessment. Scholars highlight the shift from a border-reinforcing contrastive and anxiety of influence criticism toward a transatlanticism that seeks to render the boundaries of literary or cultural criticism fluid by recognizing the permeability of national borders and complex functions of nationalistic rhetoric.[19] Practicing transatlantic criticism now is to recognize that "the true opposition . . . is not between the transatlantic and the national, but rather between the transatlantic and the exceptionalist."[20] In other words, it is a critical conversation resistant to the view that any nation is a privileged island that enjoys such cultural dominance as to be untouched by the flow of ideas, capital, and people across the sea.[21]

The Habermasian public sphere and the concept of privately oriented civic virtue trouble boundaries and reveal the latent possibility of a third sphere, discursively mediated and of sociopolitical importance. In *Virtuous Citizens* I show that this possibility of a civic identity interjected itself into the private/public, domestic/political, feminine/masculine system of binaries as a richly disruptive, fluid, and hybrid space from which a heterogeneous mix of citizens could speak back to the official sphere. Expressing anxiety and hope about the possibility of virtue in a commercial republic, these works mark the inception of a debate that continues to echo not just through scholarly work but also in modern considerations of luxury and power, class, and the efficacy of civic action in the United States and around the world.

The Shape of *Virtuous Citizens*

In the first two chapters of *Virtuous Citizens* I demonstrate the level of anxiety surrounding commerce, private virtue, and sociopolitical stability that peppered literary works during the eighteenth century, showing how this anxiety traversed the Atlantic through widely read texts. In chapter 1, I analyze economic philosophy to track how the growth of mercantilism empowered the bourgeoisie both economically and symbolically. England's international standing was increasingly credited to a combination of global trading power and a stable, virtuous middling class. This shift, rather than marking the death of civic virtue, transformed the link between private and public life, expanding the modes by which political subalterns could claim a moral right to civic participation. Exemplary of these counterpublics are the female British abolitionists who published protest poetry during the 1780s and 1790s. They are the focus of the chapter's second half. The subject of virtue, both private and public, is central to their work. Their abolitionist discourse portrays corrupt citizens whose sympathies have died as threatening the nation's moral standing. Poetry from this movement exemplifies the blending of private and public virtue in late eighteenth-century discourse, in its subject matter and in the attempt of disenfranchised citizens to effect political change through counterpublic formation.

Chapter 2 features a discussion of Gilbert Imlay, whose transatlantic life and brief moment of cultural influence offer important insights on resistance to civic activism. Published in the same decade that British female abolitionist poetry flourished, Imlay's works appeal to an audience anxious about lost political and private virtue, again portrayed as deeply intertwined. In *A Topographical Description of the Western Territory* Imlay describes the fruitful and plentiful land awaiting emigrant cultivation. His complementary novel, *The Emigrants*, portrays the United States as a refuge for virtuous English men and women seeking to escape a degrading culture. Imlay's critique of England emerges through dramatic examples of the way unjust institutions contaminate private virtue. Specifically, England's public life led to gender perversions—impotent men and unfeeling women. The United States offered hope to those who wished to maintain their most positive "natural" (gender-specific) instincts. The country's restorative power lay in the expanse of available land, which would enable the national government to gain strength through trade while providing ample space for separatist communities to avoid the corruption that accompanies commercial wealth. Imlay's imagined utopia, however, was predicated on the erasure of class status, commerce, and civic identity, all in the name of salvaging private virtue while promoting America's imperial destiny. His was a static, unsustainable response to the perceived threats to virtue that exist in a commercial society. Imlay was considered radical for his prodivorce views, but his views were politically restrictive for most citizens: *The Emigrants* is a cautionary tale against the all-consuming forces of public life, encouraging instead a return to feudalistic and chivalric modes of domesticity and expunging the possibility of political change through civic activism.

In the second half of the book I explore how writers responded to the changing landscape of public-sphere life through exploration of American politics in fiction and nonfiction. I jump to the antebellum era in chapter 3 for a discussion of historical romance novels set during the American Revolution, focusing on James Fenimore Cooper's *The Spy* and Catharine Maria Sedgwick's *The Linwoods*. These novels depict the United States as republican evolution—a corrective for Old World ills.

Cooper and Sedgwick portrayed the domestic sphere, gender relations, and family dynamics as models for national politics. These correlations, however, were used by Cooper and Sedgwick to promote two divergent visions of civic virtue. Sedgwick (like Gilbert Imlay) attached corruption to the luxury-indulging aristocratic classes; Cooper located it in the masses. These books more fully reveal how the depiction of civic life varies depending on an author's ideological foundation. Cooper, in his fiction and his nonfiction, valorized hierarchy, and his portrait of ideal leaders recalls classical definitions of civic virtue, or masculine *virtù*. Cooper's hero is an American aristocrat: a slave-owner and military general, destined to lead the passionate and irrational masses. It is these masses (nonwhite, nonmale, and non-property-owning) who are prey to corruption and who therefore threaten national stability. By contrast, in *The Linwoods* Sedgwick tells the story of an aristocratic young woman's thoughtful movement toward democratic views and presents the aristocracy as prey to immorality due to materialistic values and overly hierarchical relationships. The strongest defense of private and national virtue lies in the middle and working classes, where rational individuals can learn how to govern themselves regardless of economic or gender identity. Sedgwick's construction of virtue makes an autonomous public-sphere identity possible for all citizens, not just those with a direct line to political leadership.

In the fourth chapter I analyze the most significant early manifestation of an expanded public sphere in American history, the abolition movement, a powerful counterpublic that attracted a diverse group of participants. I open with a discussion of Harriet Martineau, a prolific British author who wrote extensively about the United States and became personally involved in the abolitionist cause. Martineau's thirty-plus years of commentary on the United States captures multiple dimensions of the debate about remaking democratic society and evolving perspectives of civic virtue and public-sphere life. In the 1830s Martineau described the US and its citizens as "embryo poets," whose faith in equality and freedom would manifest social progress; the heroes who most epitomized this faith were abolitionists, whom Martineau describes as martyrs.[22] Her paean to their sacrifices echoes rhetoric from classical republican notions of civic virtue, with an important exception. It is their commitment to freedom, an abstract political ideal, that motivates self-sacrifice and political action, rather than commitment to the nation-state. I explore how this shift manifests in two novels, Harriet Beecher Stowe's *Uncle Tom's Cabin* and Sarah Josepha Hale's *Northwood*. Even when patriotism is explicitly promoted in these novels, alternative affiliations displace ties to the nation in the formation of publics. Stowe valorizes the moral fortitude of subaltern participants in the abolition movement, while Hale promotes white transnationalism as requisite to American virtue and power. Although many during this period fought to maintain the classical definition of republican virtù (i.e., a courageous sacrifice made on behalf of the state), Martineau's, Stowe's, and Hale's work reflects a new and increasingly powerful civic life defined by imaginative and affective affiliations, linking private and public identities and inspiring transnational counterpublics.

In the conclusion, I revisit the link between the early growth of counterpublics and the shape of these communities today. Ultimately, *Virtuous Citizens* is about the civic lives of people who would not have made Pocock's or Habermas's list of central figures in the eighteenth-century public sphere. While some of the authors I discuss were not necessarily *outsiders*, I have included writers whose work had mass appeal when published; such works reflect how a broad swath of the population came to understand civic life and their own part in shaping political landscapes in England and America. Through analysis of popular poetry and novels, I dig into what the comparatively average citizen/subject was being encouraged to think about dissent. Could they be part of a virtuous, patriotic community while engaged in various forms of dissent? Could they force a change and be justified in doing so from the political margins? The literature I discuss traces how the groundwork was laid for powerful counterpublics over the course of the eighteenth and nineteenth centuries and the way these counterpublics reshaped the landscape of civic life. Counterpublics created space for more broad-based participation, giving subaltern members of the nation a sense of political efficacy. They also showed how reshaping public life can create political change, which impacts the experience of who we are in the spaces that constitute private life—the selves we imagine as possible. The modern public sphere has always constituted a vital and powerful space for those invested in addressing injustice and expanding democracy.

Private Virtue Goes Public

Civic Activism in the Middling Classes

In 1793 Anna Laetitia Barbauld responded to the English government's declaration of war against the French Republic by publishing *Sins of Government, Sins of the Nation*, in which she asks, "How far, as individuals, are we really answerable for the guilt of national sins?" Although she preaches patience, fortitude, and obedience to law, Barbauld urges all British citizens to consider themselves part of the nation and thus implicated in and responsible for ameliorating its sins. Barbauld includes herself in this moral dragnet: "We have to repent," she opines, after urging other citizens to see that "our collective capacity . . . speaks the will of the nation."[1] Barbauld wrote this tract after two bills she supported failed to pass. One aimed to overturn the Test and Corporation Acts, which restricted dissenters' political rights, and the other was an antislavery bill.[2] As a woman and a dissenter, Barbauld was doubly barred from official leadership roles in national politics. But as this pamphlet demonstrates, voting or serving the government directly was not the only path to active citizenship. The shifting economic landscape of British society, particularly the concomitant growth of the bourgeoisie with mercantile capitalism, expanded participatory inroads for citizens previously relegated to private or prepolitical identities. Economic and sociocultural changes not only propagated the mainstream bourgeois public sphere inhabited by enfranchised white men but also created a space for powerful counterpublics, communities of like-minded subalterns who used public speech to critique the government. Encouraged by political leaders to develop an emotional attachment to the nation (*Sins of Government, Sins of the Nation* responds to a national call for prayer in support of British military victory), members of the polity responded, demonstrating their investment.[3] Barbauld and other writers wielded affective nationalism in written works, seeking to expand the public's understanding of important sociopolitical issues and to empower them as citizens.[4]

Anna Laetitia Barbauld urges readers to apply domestic Christian virtue to social and political issues. She suggests that national corruption is caused by a gap between private and public morality, reflecting a significant shift in notions of civic virtue as industrialization grew and the nation-state took center stage in conceptions of political community. The role of economics in these changes has long been debated—with Hannah Arendt's and Jürgen Habermas's work looming large. In this chapter I consider its many valences, from the rhetoric of political philosophers to the anti-imperialism in much abolitionist poetry. In *The Human Condition* Arendt tracks the shifting meaning of *labor* from classical to modern times by analyzing the evolving relationship between private and public life in the republican tradition. In Greek city-states, labor was part of private life, the realm in which inequality was assumed and freedom was impossible; those conscripted to the private sphere were concerned with meeting the necessities of life. Per Aristotelian thought, freedom was only possible when these necessities were secured and the head of household entered the political realm, joining a discursive community of equally unencumbered citizens. Freedom, a meaningful life, and immortality were found in the life of the mind, not in the drudgery required to maintain physical bodies.

The relationship between labor, private life, and politics changed significantly as Western nations entered the modern era. For Arendt, these changes contribute to the loss of true privacy, a loss she mourns.[5] With the rise of modern capitalism labor moved outside the household and became part of public life, which was increasingly regulated by the social realm. Arendt uses the word *social* to describe normalizing social pressure, the coercive power of institutional consensus in a public culture driven by self-interested reputation management. For Arendt, the newly insignificant realm of privacy was once a space to develop an individual subjectivity worth publicity. Lives lived without privacy or the autonomous identity real privacy enables are inevitably shallow.[6] With an even thinner veil today between private and public life, Arendt's observation seems prescient. Scholars including Wendy Brown and Katherine Henry, however, offer compelling critiques of Arendt's schematic. Henry points out that "to situate freedom in the private realm is to imagine it in opposition to public power rather than as the exercise of public power."[7] She argues more generally that the relationship between public and private identities has long been fluid, complex, and inextricable. Building on Henry's argument, I demonstrate that the crumbling walls between domestic and public issues and the lost intimacy of private life lamented by Arendt were central to the democratization of the public sphere, a change both exposed and propelled forward by writers like Barbauld. While developing and protecting a privately constructed selfhood may have grown increasingly difficult, the shifting role of labor (or economic life) that Arendt describes allowed new claims to public subjectivity by citizens previously denied that form of social identity.

Jürgen Habermas also traces the protraction of privacy in a discussion of classical republican philosophy but with greater emphasis on the relationship between privacy, publicity, and virtue. What we now call civic virtue, Habermas argues, always required publicity: "The virtues, whose catalogue was codified by Aristotle, were ones whose test lies in the public sphere and there alone receive recognition." Hierarchy in the *oikos* (home) freed heads of household from the necessities of life and fitted them for participation in the *polis* (public). Both Arendt and Habermas demonstrate that bodies seen as historically fettered, bodies of slaves and women in particular, could not obtain autonomy or freedom. They were denied participation in the discursive polis. In Habermas's estimation, this restriction shuttered their capacity to be seen as virtuous citizens. Arendt challenges this classical notion by theorizing that any virtue requiring publicity cannot be deemed true goodness, but her contention is detached from the realities of both identity formation and the public perception of virtue/goodness.[8] Arendt ignores the concrete physical, psychological, and political ramifications when cultures relegate certain bodies to the realm of privacy, a stricture predicated on the power of shame to discourage the publicity of deviant or marginalized identities.[9]

Arendt's and Habermas's discussions of labor and economics, while illuminating challenges to a politically efficacious public sphere, fail to address the effect these changes had on marginalized peoples, whose identities provided the negative against which freedom and public virtue were understood and whose labor made such "freedom" possible for others. Arendt, Habermas, and Pocock consistently focus on the aspects of subjectivity and virtue threatened by the development of a mercantile class and civil society, rather than on its promise: the power of indeterminacy and liminality to create space for new forms of publicity, no less powerful or meaningful than the old. Arendt herself points out the ways in which members of the polis who were viewed as essentially private, including women and the poor, or who were seen as existing outside the *demos*, as was the case for slaves, were denied full humanity and freedom. But she ignores how the shifting meaning of *labor*, by obscuring the relationship between private and political life, had emancipatory potential for these state subjects. Though privacy was abraded, the changes to public life accompanying mercantile culture complicated old divisions that politically silenced these private-sphere denizens.

Labor's shifting ideological valence, in essence, created a productive obscurity. When the majority of labor moved outside the domestic sphere, it inhabited a mediated space. Necessities of life were met outside the home, and emerging economic philosophy indicated the complementary relationship between government and economic systems. Labor in the eighteenth century, while still necessary for the acquisition and maintenance of private property and the long-term stability of private life, was increasingly tied to both politics and public life. Habermas argues, "Civil society came into existence as the corollary of a depersonalized state authority. Activities and dependencies hitherto relegated to the framework of the household economy emerged from this confinement into the public sphere."[10] What did this mean for the Aristotelian conception of true freedom? Ostensibly, the ideal of unencumbered existence and freedom within a political community was no longer possible for anyone. Economic success in a bourgeois-dominant capitalist society relies upon performance outside of the home. Maintenance of private property and privacy also rely on this performance. The line between public economic life and private domestic life was blurred and thus vulnerable. This loss of privacy played a pivotal role in the growth of the public sphere. If the dominant classes struggle to delineate private from public life, disenfranchised members of the state can more easily cross that line, which they did during the eighteenth and nineteenth centuries, emerging into the public, encumbered bodies and all. Claims of freedom and autonomy obtained by having power over others in the domestic sphere, a freedom that relied on the productive labor of subalterns, were chimeras all along. They were always vulnerable. If everyone is encumbered, proclamations of freedom from necessity could no longer rationalize the exclusion of private people from the nation's public life.

When labor became a shared element of both home economy and political economics, its moral valence, rather than diminishing, expanded. As a linchpin of domestic stability and national identity, economic relationships became a lightning rod for public sphere discussions of political reform. When economics bridged domestic life and politics, questioning the morality of national economic activities became the purview of not only politicians but also the country's ethical guardians, its wives and mothers. This shift is why Nancy Fraser's concept of counterpublics is essential to understanding the evolution of modern civic life. Habermas describes the public sphere of salons, cafés, and clubs as essentially masculine (women's presence in such physical spaces was subject to silence and erasure), but the discourse arising from these spaces on the purpose and form of participation in the official realm helped usher in a civic identity that was fluidly abstract and comparatively egalitarian, laying the groundwork for the rise of counterpublics. The modern civic sphere became a space where those without official-sphere power could debate national identity, political values, and the defining features of virtuous citizenship.[11]

British abolitionism in the late eighteenth century exemplifies this change. William Wilberforce became the political face of the movement when he brought the first bill forward in 1791. This failed vote to abolish the transatlantic slave trade was propelled by a slew of interconnected subaltern communities: slaves who sued for their freedom and wrote about their experiences under slavery; Quakers who created the Society for Effecting the Abolition of the Slave Trade and roused other dissenters to join the movement; and middle-class women who wielded their religious and domestic authority to protest slavery in pamphlets, petitions, essays, and poetry.[12] Those women are the focus of my analysis because their work captures the imbrication of economics in reform rhetoric as it explores the relationship between private and public virtue. The efforts of these female poets to directly influence politics were authorized by the transformation in civic virtue that grew from an increasingly prominent middle class, whose expansion has been credited to the growth in British trade and manufacturing. Without exception, female British abolitionist poets stigmatized trade, commonly represented as the new serpent in an English Garden of Eden, precipitating the nation's fall from grace. In these poets' discourse, individuals in Britain's commercial (public) sphere are corrupted by self-interested greed, a corruption that threatens to diminish the moral standing of the nation. These poets expressed a deeply emotional response to this threat, demonstrating the patriotic investment urged by politicians who called for national days of contemplation and prayer. They wrote to save the souls of the nation and its individual citizens, protesting national policies in the name of civic virtue and suggesting through their work an inextricable link between the public and private self.

Commerce, Luxury, and Virtue: Eighteenth-Century Moral Philosophy

The work of prominent political economists illustrates the blurring of lines between private and public life. A brief survey of eighteenth-century British moral philosophy, which historians have completed from a variety of perspectives, reveals a shared set of sociocultural and political preoccupations. Philosophers debated the source of man's sociability, identifying public actions as driven by selfish desires, benevolent instincts, or some combination of the two. These conversations about human nature also interrogated the relationship between the individual citizen and the state, exploring which virtues or vices would promote the strength and stability of Great Britain. Scholars frequently trace eighteenth-century debates in moral philosophy—its preoccupation with understanding the relationship between the individual and nation, commerce and virtue—to England's Glorious Revolution, which resulted in material and ideological changes to the nation's political culture. In 1689 the Bill of Rights increased the power of parliament and significantly limited the monarchy's role in governance. This inspired a political and literary conversation in which England (though a monarchy) was frequently represented as the inheritor of classic republican empires.[13] Pocock identifies these events as pivotal in the shaping of eighteenth-century culture and thought, but he places emphasis on the shifting identity that resulted from England's attendant war. From its participation in Dutch conflicts, which accompanied William III (more commonly known as William of Orange) when he captured the English throne, England evolved into an acknowledged trading power, usurping the Dutch. "At a very rapid pace, an entity known as Trade entered the language of politics, and became something which no orator, pamphleteer, or theorist could afford to neglect and which, in an era of war, was intimately connected with the concepts of external relations and national power."[14] This expansion in trading power led to a financial revolution that ushered in an early form of credit, and the first half of the eighteenth century saw a dramatic increase in the number of government subscriptions for public funding. Individuals and private entities helped finance military and bureaucratic endeavors by loaning the government funds that acted like contemporary stocks, values rising or falling depending on the success or failure of the company—in this case, the government. In essence, well-heeled citizens could own a piece of the government as interested stakeholders.

In this more exalted realm, the monied interest enlarged their presence in political affairs via such investments,[15] while in the mercantile realm the middling classes grew their public profile through economic gains.[16] These changes were explored and promoted by Adam Smith, David Hume, and their cohort, which has been substantiated by historians who have analyzed the role of luxury in eighteenth-century social and political discourse. The first half of the eighteenth century saw the rise not only of manufacturing and merchant capitalism but also the attendant rise of a middle class with purchasing power.[17] The growth in manufacturing and trade activity throughout the century led to an increase in wages, one that peaked in the 1760s and 1770s.[18] This increased income made it possible for the middling classes to participate in the consumption of luxury items, which in turn drove production of nonessential goods. Maxine Berg declares this a "product revolution," during which consuming specific commodities once beyond their reach became a way for the rising bourgeoisie to establish their public identities.[19]

All of these changes constituted an increased middle-class stock in the nation, as various writers characterized economic consumption as essential to national prosperity and growth. Bernard Mandeville represents the most extreme proponent of this proluxury perspective; however, David Hume and Adam Smith also trumpeted the positive results of growth in manufacturing and consumerism.[20] In a 1731 pamphlet Daniel Defoe declared that the "trading, middling sort of people . . . are the life of our whole commerce . . . it is by their expensive, generous, free way of living, that the home consumption is rais'd to such a bulk, as well of our own, as of foreign production." This wider circulation of luxuries created a "populous, rich, fruitful" nation.[21] Positive exhortations by Defoe and others on the growing wealth of Britain did not assuage the entrenched fear that trade, and in particular luxury, enervated the moral faculties, but the expansion of merchant capitalism and increased purchasing power of the bourgeoisie changed this conversation in meaningful ways. The increased public prominence of the middling classes laid the foundation for a conception of civic virtue that placed nonaristocratic citizens at its center.

The Earl of Shaftesbury and Bernard Mandeville, two early British entrants into debates about luxury, commerce, individual desires, and sociability, sit at opposite ideological ends of eighteenth-century moral philosophy.[22] Shaftesbury promoted a definition of virtue that lauds man's natural desire to benefit society. Mandeville presented an image of man as driven by selfish desires, with any benefit to society an unintended result of self-interested participation in commerce. In *The Fable of the Bees*, a highly controversial book, Mandeville says of Shaftesbury, "The attentive Reader, who perused the foregoing part of this Book, will soon perceive that two Systems cannot be more opposite than his Lordship's and mine."[23] Mandeville refers here to Shaftesbury's insistence that virtue is defined by the individual's choice to act for the public good. Shaftesbury, whose various essays were collected in *Characteristicks of Men, Manners, Opinions, Times*, builds his definition of virtue through a comparison of animal actions to human ones. While animals can be said to practice "goodness" by fulfilling their instinctual drives in situations such as the protection of young, these actions should not be described as "virtuous." Virtuous action requires a moral consciousness and "Trial or Exercise of the Heart."[24] Like many before and after him, Shaftesbury argues that virtue requires an active choice and struggle. This struggle often takes place in the heart or spirit of individuals as they face fear or consciously sacrifice their own interests for the greater good. Using the capacity for reason that separates man from beast, the individual who develops an understanding of right and wrong in the context of social need, then acts upon it, demonstrates virtue.[25]

Bernard Mandeville's work explodes this view of human nature. F. B. Kaye contends that Mandeville's work has been perennially misunderstood by readers who forget it is a satire meant to expose hypocrisy rather than a tract meant to offer a methodology for creating ideal citizens—but this view elides the book's cultural significance. Mandeville made waves, and while elements of the work may be satirical, he was sincerely engaged in understanding the relationship between morality, economic life, and national prosperity. The impact of Mandeville's book has rightfully carved a place for *The Fable of the Bees* in historical and literary discussions of eighteenth-century political philosophy. It "attracted well over a hundred refutations or detailed condemnations before the end of the century."[26] The list of responders reads like a who's-who of eighteenth-century political thought. The 1723 edition included an essay arguing against the funding of poor schools for working-class children that incited vigorous response from social reformers.[27] *The Fable of the Bees* even received juridical censure: It was "presented before the Grand Jury of Middlesex and there declared a public nuisance. The presentment of the Jury claimed that the *Fable* intended to disparage religion and virtue as detrimental to society, and to promote vice as a necessary component of a well-functioning state."[28]

Mandeville responded to this seemingly common perception, in his view a misperception: "If laying aside all worldly Greatness and Vain-Glory, I should be ask'd where I thought it was most probable that Men might enjoy true Happiness, I would prefer a small peaceable Society, in which Men, neither envy'd nor esteem'd by Neighbours, should be contented to live upon the Natural Product of the Spot they inhabit, to a vast Multitude abounding in Wealth and Power, that should always be conquering others by their Arms Abroad, and debauching themselves by Foreign Luxury at Home."[29] Mandeville's response crystallizes the central purport of his book: vice is not the path to peace, contentment, and individual happiness. In fact, Mandeville challenges the popular assumption that peace and contentment are natural human drives or valuable goals for the nation. Mandeville was responding to moralizing work that decried vice and expounded selflessness as the ultimate virtue but failed to acknowledge the ability of self-interest and vicious desires, in particular the desire to obtain luxuries, to increase national prosperity. His express purpose was "to expose the Unreasonableness and Folly of those, that desirous of being an opulent and flourishing People, and wonderfully greedy after all the Benefits they can receive as such, are yet always murmuring at and exclaiming against those Vices and Inconveniences, that from the Beginning of the World to this present Day, have been inseparable from all Kingdoms and States that ever were fam'd for Strength, Riches, and Politeness, at the same time."[30] If you cure the vices, Mandeville's poem and essays declare, you sap the vital energy from society that propels men to produce more goods and acquire more wealth, ventures that create the need for lawyers, judges, merchants, and artisans, and that throughout history have been the impetus for civilization's progress. In his effort to prove this point, Mandeville presents a rather dark view of human nature, depicting men as driven solely by self-interest. In the poem, as soon as man becomes virtuous and society peaceful, houses fall into disrepair as nature runs wild, the arts die, and industry grinds to a halt because these activities are motivated by vanity, greed, envy, and other vicious passions.[31] Mandeville's work presents all those who participate in commercial life, through industry or consumption, as vital to national interests. In some ways, Barbauld herself might have applauded Mandeville, or at least related to the satire within his work. She calls on those who defend imperialism and war to stop hiding behind proclamations of virtuous intent and religious justification: "Let us lay aside the grimace of hypocrisy, and stand up for what we are, and boldly profess, like the emperor of old, that every thing is sweet from which money is extracted, and that we know better than to deprive ourselves of a gain for the sake of a fellow-creature."[32] Barbauld's and Mandeville's works promote the idea that, invariably, there is a relationship between the economic system/actions of the nation and the virtue of its citizens.

Another important political implication of Mandeville's work is that the advances in civilization, which he argues have improved the quality of life for even the poorest British citizens, were built on the industry of society's "middling" classes and the rise of the bourgeoisie.[33] The role played by class in Mandeville's work is essential to understanding its place in eighteenth-century political and economic philosophy. Mandeville's position directly counters what he considered a privileged idealism typified by the Earl of Shaftesbury. In Mandeville's view, Shaftesbury could ponder the beauties of virtue and characterize man as naturally altruistic only because of his landed, aristocratic status, which helped him maintain a safe distance from the daily buzzing of the British hive.[34] This Aristotelian ideal of civic virtue rests precariously on freedom from meeting the bodily necessities of life, a freedom gained by reliance on other people's labor. Mandeville's book is written from the perspective of the comparatively encumbered "middling sort." Mandeville was a physician, and his references to various members of the hive focus on this sector of society: the doctors, lawyers, merchants, and artisans who work for their income, and the wives who participate in economics by managing household spending.

In *The Fable of the Bees* Mandeville effectively considers the classical republican tradition of civic virtue as irrelevant, arguing that beneficial social behavior could result from vicious desires. While Mandeville clearly tapped into fears about the power of self-interest, the perspective in *Fable* was a fringe view. For the majority of writers laboring to understand virtue's role in a shifting economic landscape, it could not be discounted as either unnecessary or unimportant to national identity. Two of the most influential mid-eighteenth-century moral philosophers offered reflections on society that place the middling and manufacturing population at the center of national progress without denying the possibility and importance of civic virtue. David Hume and Adam Smith offer complex middle ground between Shaftesbury's and Mandeville's antagonistic philosophies.

In "Of Refinement in the Arts," originally titled "Of Luxury," Hume attempts to bring both the alarmist and idealizing views of luxury down to earth. One of Hume's central points is that *luxury*, like *morality*, is a relative term. What is considered luxury and what is considered vicious vary both historically and geographically. Luxury only leads to vice when overindulgence by either the individual or the nation results in personal ruin or neglect of moral responsibilities. Hume places responsibility for virtue and vice in the individual's and the government's use, or abuse, of luxury and urges readers to recognize the value in mercantile growth. The advance of industry and the arts that accompany increased wealth and luxury, in Hume's view, are essential components of the move away from feudalism and toward increased liberty for all. In this essay and "Of Commerce," Hume touts the inextricable relationship between increased commerce and luxury, the humanity of citizens, and the strength of the nation itself. Three key terms, repeated throughout "Of Refinement," structure Hume's claim: "industry, knowledge, and humanity."[35] Hume uses "humanity" to describe morally positive behavior in concert with the larger community. This humanity, along with increased knowledge, occurs as a result of the industry that brings men together through trade. Through his delineation of mercantile culture, Hume challenges nostalgia for the martial civic virtues of classical republics. In modern England, Hume argues, industry replaces war to keep the mind and body active. War dehumanized people, making it difficult for them to rejoin the everyday operations of a community. Rather than causing vice, the enjoyment of luxury, whether in the form of arts or commodities, encourages industry and discourages idleness in men.[36] While Hume does not claim in these essays that wholly virtuous motives drive mercantile productivity, he does argue that it positively impacts the virtue of both individual participants and the nation as a whole.

Hume's philosophy is informed by his belief that increased economic equality is essential to the growth of individual liberties. In "Of Commerce" Hume traces the stages of progress from a life of subsistence to increases in agricultural production, to manufacturing and expansion of trade. Hume argues that when this final stage has been reached, a nation becomes not only more prosperous but also a more hospitable site for liberty. The civilian need not give his life in war to serve the country. If his right to property is protected and he is motivated to labor by a desire for luxuries, he can contribute to the nation's strength through taxes.[37] The nation's strength, then, lies not in the martial attributes of its most heroic citizens (an elite few) but instead in its economic power, which proceeds from the industry of its general population. Conversely, society without the arts/luxuries produces two classes of men, enslaved farmers and petty tyrants: "But where luxury nourishes commerce and industry, the peasants, by a proper cultivation of the land, become rich and independent; while the tradesmen and merchants acquire a share of the property, and draw authority and consideration to that middling rank of men, who are the best and firmest basis of public liberty."[38] For Hume liberty is essential to virtue, and a growing middle class is the best guarantor of increased liberty. While Shaftesbury parrots classical notions of republican virtue and Mandeville critiques them, David Hume and Adam Smith present arguments for a modern conception of civic virtue that shifts responsibility for progress from nonlaboring landowners to the middling classes.

Not long after Hume published the collection of essays containing "Of Refinement" and "Of Commerce," Smith produced *The Theory of Moral Sentiments*.[39] Though he covers large swaths of historical moral thought and includes detailed descriptions of contemporary behaviors, Smith ultimately focuses on how sympathy and a desire for recognition figure in people's morals and actions. Smith includes a discussion of class that complements Hume's work, one that places the working and middle classes at the heart of English culture and national progress. The wealthy receive automatic approval from society. The lower and middling classes develop the virtues of "patience, industry, fortitude, and application of thought," suiting them better for leadership positions in the government.[40] Though he does not expressly condemn the aristocracy as morally corrupt, Smith suggests here and elsewhere that wealth without industry most threatens the virtues, a philosophy that clearly favors the nonaristocratic classes as model citizens, more critical to the nation's stability and moral tenor than the landed aristocracy. It is natural to admire the wealthy because they appear to have more closely approached the ideal life, Smith acknowledges, but this is "the great and most universal cause of the corruption of our moral sentiments."[41] As recipients of an admiration that sometimes errs on the side of obsequiousness, the wealthy are allowed to overindulge and flout the country's laws; they are held to a lower standard of ethical civic behavior than other citizens. By contrast, men who are required to earn their own living must cultivate a positive communal reputation by developing admirable manners and habits; honesty is the best policy for the laboring citizen in a mercantile democracy.[42] Taken together, Smith's and Hume's economic philosophies suggest an increasingly prominent and sociopolitically significant role for the economic realm, the public sphere, and the middle-class citizens who circulate there.

Civic Virtue in the Middling Classes: Private and Public, Masculine and Feminine

Hume's and Smith's view that national morality sat most comfortably on the shoulders of Britain's middling classes offers important insight into shifting notions of private and public virtue during the eighteenth century. Smith argues that self-denial and self-government are the foundational qualities required to achieve them. Although Smith is not the focus of his analysis, Pocock argues that the emergence of the protestant ethic (i.e., virtue as self-denial in the form of frugality and other domestic behaviors) was a direct response to the underlying sense that with the growth of commercial society, civic virtue would inevitably fall to corruption.[43] Economic philosophers like Hume and Smith dismissed classical, martial notions of virtue as obsolete referents for eighteenth-century economic and cultural life. This stance created, in Pocock's view, an alienation from history and from a stable ground for concepts of self: "Once property was seen to have a symbolic value, expressed in coin or in credit, the foundations of personality themselves appeared imaginary or at best consensual: the individual could exist . . . only at the fluctuating value imposed upon him by his fellows."[44] Pocock concludes that the swift growth of a credit economy, in which value relative to coin was symbolic rather than intrinsic, required men to rely on both imagination and fiction in their daily lives. He represents this economic shift as an elegiac moment and the work of promarket moralists as failed compensation for the loss of a stable and grounded basis for civic virtue. The onset of credit, according to Pocock, signed civic virtue's death warrant: embracing a mercantile, credit-based economy meant accepting corruption in public life and reimagining the government as responsible for controlling the spread and impact of man's vices.[45] But Pocock's interpretation does not deal adequately with the alternative forms of civic virtue presented by writers during this period, whether economic theorists or popular authors. Barbauld's work alone demonstrates that people living through these economic and social changes were actively redefining national morality and civic life.

I am not the first to challenge Pocock's conclusion. Shelley Burtt, offering important revisions, defines civic virtue as the sphere "in which individuals participate, to a greater or lesser extent, in the shaping of their collective destiny. . . . Civic virtue names those dispositions of the individual that make him or her a good citizen of this sort of regime—that is, that lead him or her to engage in the sort of public (and private) behavior that enable a civic mode of life both to survive and to flourish."[46] Burtt highlights the diffusion of civic virtue's boundaries. Rather than disappearing, opportunities to see oneself as capable of a virtuous and impactful civic identity expanded. The spread of power in the economic realm described positively by Hume and Smith, the opportunity for private individuals and organizations to become supporters of the government, and the shift away from monarchical toward parliamentary politics all signal an increased sense of participatory opportunities for British citizens over the course of the eighteenth century. In addition, the emphasis placed on commerce and trade's role in the strength of the nation, as opposed to a definition that focused on martial activities or the elite landed class, imbued the bourgeoisie with an increased practical and ideological role in the nation. Successful merchants and traders could see themselves, by striving for their own financial benefit, as promoting the interests of England. Their public and private lives were deeply intertwined.

These changes led to and informed literary responses to civic issues during the revolutionary-heady 1790s. Eighteenth-century abolitionists typify the extent to which evolving ideals of civic virtue helped marginalized citizens find a voice in political debates. This vision of civic virtue's evolution is supported not only by contemporary moral philosophers but also by the many literary productions that demonstrated a complex intermingling between private interest and domestic life, on the one hand, and public discourse about morality and national politics on the other. Eighteenth-century female authors who engaged in avowedly political movements, including abolitionist poets, epitomize the mixing of personal and public identities. For female citizens, understood as essentially private by most eighteenth-century cultural arbiters, textual participation in political debate represented a boundary crossing. This blurring and bending of boundaries is equally visible in the content of their poems, which argue for political action in response to vicious assaults on both domestic life and national virtue.

Pocock acknowledges the discourse of protestant ethics extant during the eighteenth century (a key contributor to the heightened emphasis on private virtue), but he dismisses these efforts as failed consolations. The explosion of discourse describing private virtues as publicly relevant deserves more attention. Smith's work, for one, suggests an evolution in civic virtue that straddles the line between private/feminine virtues and classical masculine virtù, epitomized by bravery during times of war. Smith describes a tradition of moral theory in which the passions are divided into two separate categories, each requiring a distinct form of self-command. The first category includes fear and anger, both of which require a resolute but temporary self-mastery. These passions excite the strongest reactions and therefore require a more powerful fortitude to control them. The second category includes the daily temptations to indulge in pleasures known to be detrimental to virtue, such as love of ease and pleasure: "The command of the former was, by the ancient moralists above alluded to, denominated fortitude, manhood, and strength of mind; that of the latter, temperance, decency, modesty, and moderation."[47] In Smith's examples, self-mastery excites the highest level of esteem in observers, even when demonstrated by a thief on the scaffold who refuses to be cowed. These examples demonstrate the tradition of classical virtue Pocock's work so thoroughly explores (i.e., bravery in the face of death), wherein the most valued public virtues are those that suit men for war or political leadership.

Smith never refers directly to women in this discussion. Even when women are implied, he folds them into non-gender-specific descriptions. A comparative list of virtues ascribes the first to manhood and fails to gender the complementary set, leaving little room for confusion. The second set of qualities, although certainly applicable and admirable in men, according to Smith can also be achieved by those politically consigned to the private sphere, the "humbler" peoples for whom chastity is an essential trait. "It is from the unremitting steadiness of those gentler exertions of self-command, that the amiable virtue of chastity, that the respectable virtues of industry and frugality, derive all that sober lustre which attends them. The conduct of all those who are contented to walk in the humble paths of private and peaceable life, derives from the same principle the greater part of the beauty and grace which belong to it; a beauty and grace, which, though much less dazzling, is not always less pleasing than those which accompany the more splendid actions of the hero, the statesman, or the legislator."[48] While one implication of this passage is that only those who can obtain masculine virtù are fit to be leaders, Hume's and Smith's suggestion that national prosperity and liberty are in the hands of the middling classes gives the softer virtues increased public significance.

Jane Rendall points out that Smith's "relocation of the pursuit of virtue within the private sphere, at its heart the life of the family and the moral inspiration of women," was a response to fear regarding the death of a public sector separate from economic transactions.[49] Taking Rendall's analysis one step further, if the greatest threat to national strength is dishonesty and fraud in the commercial world, self-mastery in the face of death is less essential to sociopolitical stability than the practice of what Smith identified as the "less dazzling" virtues: "temperance, decency, modesty, and moderation," as well as "chastity," "industry and frugality."[50] These virtues, which Smith asserts add "beauty and grace" to private life, are commonly ascribed to women. Equally important, these virtues are not attached to either martial or political identities. Redefining virtues along domestic lines, whether intended or not, offered a civic identity to citizens without legitimized political clout. Rendall argues that during this period, "Increasingly, citizenship came to be seen as resting not on virtue, but on rights, the rights of the individual, both natural and contractual."[51] Though Rendall's contention is broadly true, the language of virtue, more specifically debates that (re)codified the ideals of republican virtue, continued to play a prominent role in efforts to expand or limit the authority of middling and marginalized citizens. While Smith's heroes and statesmen obtain classical masculine virtù, the vast majority of British citizens (the middling classes that Smith, Hume, and Mandeville consider central to British liberty and prosperity) could see themselves as exemplifying a form of virtue that linked their private life to national interests. Smith often focuses on the moralizing power of reputation-management in an open market; the implications of his philosophy are much broader. The feminine and domestic virtues are represented as publicly impactful and central to the modern democratic nation. As a result, middle-class British women could see themselves as exemplars of civic virtue through management of the domestic sphere, thereby authorized by their feminine virtues to participate in public sphere debate regarding national politics.

Abolitionist Poetry as Civic Speech

Generally, scholars see the rising protest against British slavery as a response to historical events that led to national self-reflection. Building on Eric Williams's groundbreaking reevaluation of British abolitionism, Christopher Leslie Brown claims the American Revolution played a primary role in activating British antislavery by fomenting debate regarding liberty and national virtue and, more specifically, by drawing attention to the ways in which imperialism and slavery problematized British self-representation. Brown sees the abolition of slavery as an effort to gain moral capital, which the British then used (or spent) to justify expansion of the British Empire. Female abolitionist poetry confirms the extent to which imperialism was a source of anxiety for abolitionists. It also suggests that not all participants in the movement wanted to buoy the imperial cause. Citizens involved in abolitionism sought "to think of themselves as Christian, moral, and free," but more was at stake for marginalized subjects than increased self-regard. Claiming a deep understanding of and the right to defend civic virtue was a way to center themselves in political debates. Describing nineteenth-century American authors, Karen E. Weyler demonstrates the extent to which marginalized citizens used print to "validate their claims for identity," to acquire "symbolic and cultural capital," and to belong "to something bigger than themselves."[52] For female abolitionists, gaining moral capital was an essential step toward greater participation in national affairs.

John Kane's work explores the role of virtue in garnering and maintaining political power, or in his terms political "capital," as distinguished from moral capital: "Mere money, then, is not necessarily financial capital, nor skill necessarily human capital, nor knowledge necessarily intellectual capital, nor a network of social relationships necessarily social capital. They become so only when mobilized for the sake of tangible, exterior returns. Capital, in other words, is wealth in action. The same holds for moral capital. Moral capital is moral prestige—whether of an individual, an organization or a cause—in useful service."[53] Because of the role moral capital plays in politics and hierarchical social systems, analyzing broad portrayals of private and public virtue is essential to understanding the modes in which marginalized subjects work to become recognized citizens, to emerge out of the demos. Jacques Ranciere defines politics as "a process, not a sphere" and contends that "to be of the demos is to be outside the count, to have no speech to be heard." Ranciere argues that democracy is always emergent, never a fully realized system. For democracy to survive there must be "an infinite openness to the Other or the newcomer"; in the late eighteenth century, female abolitionist poets represent such a group. Their work staged "scenes of dissensus," speaking in a way that challenged standing categories of virtue, gender, and patriotism, and "making themselves seen [and] heard as speaking subjects."[54]

Scholars continue to debate whether the feminization of eighteenth-century civic virtue was liberating for female subjects. Dana Harrington argues that the move to disentangle commerce and corruption prompted eighteenth-century nonaristocratic intellectuals to establish the home, and the woman within it, as a moralizing influence to save her husband's soul and oversee the moral education of their male children. This model required women, for the sake of protecting their virtue, to remain strictly private, to think of themselves not as citizens but instead as subjects whose greatest virtue was submission to the will of others. In Harrington's estimate, the ideological presence of femininity and domesticity in civic discourse only served to maintain the ideal of the apolitical, private Englishwoman.[55] In support of her claim, she cites Hannah More, who for Harrington is an exemplar of eighteenth-century women who "drew upon liberal ideals to support the moral roles that worked to deny them more extensive participation in public spheres."[56] More, however, is a conflicted choice to exemplify the subject status occupied by the privatized female citizen. Whereas her didactic work explicitly promoted the submissive feminine ideal, she was an active public-sphere participant, conversing on political and cultural topics with prominent politicians, philosophers, and fellow authors. She wrote tracts that lionized separate sphere ideology, but More's participation in these conversations and her publication of abolitionist poetry made her a well-known voice in multiple sociopolitical debates. Separate-sphere proponents argued that the moral health of the nation meant keeping political and commercial exchanges out of the home, thus reifying the private/public divide. More's career demonstrates this contradiction was less a reflection of reality than an effort to shape it: "even the most conventional British women would come to accept that formal exclusion from active citizenship did not exclude them from playing a patriotic role—and a political role of a kind."[57] Hannah More, known for her sermonizing, did not practice what she preached.

When private virtue became central to concepts of national strength, creating a stream of influence that ran from hearth to parliament halls, it was not possible to slam the house door before pieces of commerce and parliament found their way right back to that hearth. In the amorphous and liminal civic zone where the private and political intermingle, commerce's impact on virtue continued to occupy the minds of Britain's citizens, a fact vividly evident in abolitionist rhetoric, including that of Hannah More. Female abolitionist poets of the late eighteenth century exemplify the hybridization of spheres and ideologies authorized by the evolution in civic virtue. Moira Ferguson and Ann K. Mellor have argued that female political poetry in this era resulted from changing religious ideology, a dissenting movement that encouraged political protest and the inclusion in some sects of female preachers who spoke publicly about sociopolitical problems.[58] While religious ideology is certainly an important cultural precursor to such work, the growing national role of middle-class citizens and changing landscape of civic virtue were also instrumental in the emergence of female activism, poetic or otherwise.[59] The form of religious activity discussed by Ferguson and Mellor is another manifestation of the broader shift in public sphere access. While More, Barbauld, and other female abolitionist poets (such as Ann Yearsley, Harriet and Maria Falconar, and Mary Birkett Card)[60] legitimated their political calls to action by speaking on behalf of Christian virtue, this intervention was just one way their poetry helped dismantle the discursive division of spheres.[61] Though all were Christian, these poets were not united by religious affiliation: Card was a Quaker, Yearsley an Anglican, More a converted evangelical, and Barbauld a dissenter.[62] Their poetry is united by sentimental protest against the institution of slavery as well as shared imagery that explores the relationship between private and national virtue. The forms of community building and calls to evangelize that grew out of Protestantism influenced many activists during this period. Rallying around a shared political cause created new transdenominational counterpublics.

Through critiques of British involvement in the slave trade, female abolitionist poets further reinforced the inability to separate commercial and political activity from private interests. As writers explored these concerns, there was no sense of a protected space or of impenetrable barriers between the domestic and the political. One of the most apparent manifestations of private domestic life in abolitionist texts occurs in the poets' invocation of romantic and familial love. This trope is widely discussed by scholars who focus on literary representations of American slavery, particularly in sentimental novels such as *Uncle Tom's Cabin*.[63] American novelists described the physical and emotional impact of slavery within national borders and domestic spaces; British poets imagined African romantic and familial ties on distant shores. These scenes serve multiple purposes: they argue for a shared humanity between Englishmen and slaves, add potent sentimental drama to the political conversation, and at times critique slave traders and owners for showing less humanity, understood as social conscience and sentimental connections, than the slaves. In *A Poem on the Inhumanity of the Slave Trade*, Ann Yearsley tells the story of Luco and the woman he loves, Incalada. Dragged away from her by slave traders, Luco thinks only of his father and Incalada. Incalada dies of grief, and Luco is tortured on a sugar plantation, struck blind, and then burned alive by a cruel master. Luco shows extreme fortitude in the face of torture, a heroic virtue inspired by domestic affections. Yearsley's poem suggests that heroic virtue—Luco's stoicism in the face of cruelty, mirroring the bravery Adam Smith describes and attaches to statesmen and military leaders—is dependent upon private attachments.[64] At the same time, Yearsley illustrates the hypocrisy of masters and merchants who rely on custom and legal sanction to excuse vicious behavior. The narrator addresses a "crafty merchant" who refutes abolitionist sentiment by claiming the slave trade helps feed his children, then imagines that merchant's anguish if his own wife, children, or aging mother were put up for sale.[65] Luco's heroic love and desire for a family contrasts with the merchant's mimicry of familial devotion to achieve greed-driven self-interest. While such sentimental domestic scenes may have been designed to evoke readers' sympathy, works like Yearsley's also rewrite civic virtue by demonstrating the complex ways public identity relies on the demonstration of a private selfhood, whether sincere or craftily performed to serve political ends. Yearsley's merchant exposes the dark side of Adam Smith's faith in reputation-management to serve a moralizing purpose: the threat that public opinion, rather than inspiring virtue, will be manipulated for self-interested purposes.

The rhetoric of domestic tragedy was also used to suggest the degrading impact slavery had on the British. Moira Ferguson convincingly argues that eighteenth-century abolitionist poetry created an enduring image of Africans as "unproblematized, simpleminded victims" with the ultimate goal of reinstating Britain's standing as the global center of Christian virtue.[66] Focusing on nineteenth-century slave narratives, Ramesh Mallipeddi offers a worthwhile counterpoint, noting that sentimentalism itself "can be read as a protest against the forces of capitalist modernity" (i.e., commodification, abstraction, and instrumentalization).[67] Ferguson and Mallipeddi are correct. While many of these poems create or reconstitute the trope of Africans as fundamentally emotional rather than rational, they concurrently challenge readers to prioritize emotion and human relationships over pragmatic capitalistic pursuits.[68]

In these poems, British participation in slavery poses a cultural and spiritual threat: a life of avarice will damage the Englishman's Christian soul. That being said, the most prominent message in these poems is not of religious failure but of national political failure. The poets hold the government and merchants responsible for Britain's moral decay. In *Slavery, a Poem*, Christian virtue fortifies English identity by maintaining citizens' commitment to Liberty and Freedom, personified and directly addressed in the first two stanzas. More presents slavery, or the denial of liberty, as an act against Nature, propagated by a nation that has forgotten its values:

> Shall Britain, where the soul of Freedom reigns,
> Forge chains for others she herself disdains?
> Forbid it, Heaven! O let the nations know
> The liberty she loves she will bestow.[69]

This theme, which portrays Britain as the defender of liberty while bemoaning the hypocrisy of national support for the slave trade, is notable in other works. The poems of Harriet Falconar and Anna Laetitia Barbauld potently represent the threat posed by commerce and avarice, not just to English society but also to the idea of Britishness through inclusion of the Britannia mythos. In *Poems on Slavery*, written at age fourteen in concert with her seventeen-year-old sister, Harriet Falconar creates a vivid allegory for the relationship between imperial trade and the British citizen. After listing the intellectual and moral heroes who represent Britain's true promise as a nation—Shakespeare, Milton, Swift, Pope, and Newton—Falconar warns against the stultifying effects of greed:

> In Britain's paradise, by freedom made,
> The tree of commerce spread's its ample shade . . .
> And wealth bright glitters on each golden bough.[70]

Britain's citizen submits to temptation, plucks the sparkling fruit, and falls into an emotional stupor that silences his sympathetic moral conscience. One branch contains "the richest gems of India," a reference that lays the blame for moral devolution at the feet of imperial trade as a whole rather than on slavery alone. Falconar calls on the British government to awaken her sleeping citizens with evident nostalgia for a paradisiacal, preimperial past.

Such nostalgia and belief in a true English identity, threatened in the late eighteenth century by involvement in the slave trade, is equally evident in Barbauld's writings. Barbauld deploys the metaphor of disease to warn against the impact on the country's citizens. Dwelling on idyllic scenes of rural village life, where laboring men and women shine with the innocent glow of "thriving industry, and faithful love," Barbauld warns that participation in the slave trade will allow a "spreading leprosy" to infiltrate the British national body. The corruption of slavery dulls the emotions of planters and their wives: Barbauld describes the "placid" demeanor of one such wife as she tortures her slaves. Barbauld contrasts the corrupted "Briton" with the "blooming maids, and frolic swains" of a thriving English town.[71] This imagery offers a dramatic reflection on the power of political and commercial actions to affect the domestic life and sensibility of average citizens. Britain's people and reputation, Barbauld warns, are threatened by the inability of Parliament to abolish the slave trade and control the moral infection arising from international commerce:

> Stern Independence from his glebe retires,
> And anxious Freedom eyes her drooping fires;
> By foreign wealth are British morals chang'd
> And Afric's sons, and India's, smile aveng'd.[72]

Barbauld suggests that while politicians may worry about the bloody revenge of a slave rebellion, the damage to Britain's symbolic stature as the home of liberty, freedom, and virtue is the more significant loss.[73]

Her poem captures the private, affective resonance of national belonging. Lost faith in the nation is not just a public issue. Abolitionist poems center civic virtue and show the extent to which individual subjectivity formed through and within a national ethos. In rhetoric similar to Barbauld's, Mary Birkett Card explains that her need to speak publicly derives from her patriotism, which she describes as a passionate, even religious, attachment to being English:

> That sacred zeal which in my bosom glows,
> Claims a strong interest in thy weal or woes.
> Oft, when the passing hours of childhood ran,
> How was I pleas'd thy glorious acts to scan!
> Oft too, with transport, would I learn thy fame,
> And boast the lustre of the English name.[74]

Card's nostalgia for a youthful attachment to England and the pride of identification with an honored homeland, is dramatically severed by the country's involvement in gore and oppression. Barbauld's and Card's poems, in these moments, expose a site of confluence between public and private. Both poets imply that a personal affective attachment to national identity authorizes their work within the public sphere.

This new conception of civic virtue that saw private and public morality as interconnected drove civic activism by promulgating cultural anxiety.[75] The sins of the nation could infiltrate and corrupt the private sphere. The British slave trader, sympathies hardened by the corrupting powers of avarice, carried back to England a moral infection that threatened the individual domestic sympathies and the nation's international power. In British abolitionist poetry the lines between private and public, personal and political, domestic and national are blurred beyond recognition: influence runs dangerously and productively in every direction. Although these poets often relied on domestic and sentimental tropes to protest slavery, making use of a separate-sphere ideology that granted women authority within the private realm, they also wrote with authority on the subject of British national identity, commerce, and public virtue. Ann Yearsley and Anna Laetitia Barbauld, in particular, strike an assertive tone while admonishing politicians for failing to protect and uphold British ideals. Yearsley rebukes Parliament:

> Speak, ye few
> Who fill Britannia's senate, and are deem'd
> The fathers of your country! Boast your laws,
> Defend the *honour* of a land so fall'n.[76]

Yearsley boldly implies that the fathers of the country are failing, so the mothers must intercede. Barbauld ends her poem by asking the Senate how they will be remembered by history:

> But seek no more to break a Nation's fall,
> For ye have sav'd yourselfs—and that is all.
> Succeeding times your struggles, and their fate,
> With mingled shame and triumph shall relate,
> While faithful History, in her various page,
> Marking the features of this motley age,
> To shed a glory, and to fix a stain,
> Tells how you strove, and that you strove in vain.[77]

Scholars have emphasized the complicity of these poets in separate-sphere discourse, but the power of these poems derives both from a privately oriented moral authority and a politically forceful urgency. These poets sampled from discourses of domesticity, commerce, politics, and virtue to encourage specific actions on the part of the government and of other citizens. For example, Mary Birkett Card urged women to boycott tea and other goods tainted by the practice of slavery. Alongside these qualities, the poets' fervent emotional attachment to national identity exemplifies the inextricable nature of private and public virtue at the end of the eighteenth century. These female writers, authorized by the evolution of the public sphere, helped redefine civic identity in at least two important ways: (1) by representing the intrinsic relationship between private and public virtue, and (2) by imbuing their political protests with the rhetoric of civic pride, what is now called patriotism. There is no question these female authors saw themselves as an important part of the civic body.

Conclusion

In a collection of tales for children written with her brother, John Aikin, Anna Laetitia Barbauld offers a revised vision of "True Heroism" that reflects the changing status of the middling classes and the evolution of civic virtue. Barbauld first describes the exploits of classical heroes: Achilles, Alexander the Great, and Charles of Sweden, together admired for "that high courage which seemed to set them above all sensations of fear and rendered them capable of the most extraordinary actions." She then describes these political and military leaders collectively as a "ferocious savage," a man driven by the "love of glory," and a "tyrannical" and "unfeeling" leader who cared only for power: "Self, you see, was the spring of all their conduct; and a *selfish man* can never be a hero."[78] Barbauld's story interrogates the value of classical republican virtue, masculine virtù, which holds up military and political leadership as the true venues for civic heroism.

Who is a hero in Barbauld's tale? After criticizing the exploits of these famous military leaders, she tells the stories of two contemporary men: Mr. Howard, a doctor who dedicated his life to easing the suffering of prisoners, and the even more humble Tom, whose father was an unnamed bricklayer who took to drink and abandoned his family. Tom's purpose in life is to help his poor mother; he cares more for her well-being than he does for his own. After breaking his leg at work, Tom suffers in silence and, overcoming his physical pain, promises to recover quickly so his mother need not worry. Virtù, the masculine and martial classical civic virtue, is critiqued and transformed—but not entirely abandoned—in Barbauld's tale. The fortitude to withstand personal pain and the willingness to sacrifice all (including his life) for a greater purpose are evident in Tom's actions. But his greater purpose is familial love, not political or military power. It is virtue inspired and performed within the private, domestic sphere by a member of the populace who must work, a citizen who will never enjoy the Aristotelian ideal of freedom from labor, unencumbered by biological and practical needs. Barbauld characterizes Tom's form of virtue as an evolution, a sign of progress in sociopolitical values.

Over the course of the eighteenth century, political and social philosophers, encouraged by the rising role commerce played in understanding national strength, redefined civic virtue to focus on the general populace rather than elite political and military leaders. As the modes for participating in civic life increased, in particular through the expansion of a print public sphere, access burgeoned to the role of a *virtuous citizen*. The growing public role of the middling classes meant that British Toms and Dr. Howards, men who cultivated private virtues through domestic duty, could (and in Barbauld's eyes, should) define national virtue. It also meant that politically marginalized citizens, women like Anna Laetitia Barbauld and contemporary female writers who continued to be described as essentially private, were ideologically authorized to participate in these debates. Barbauld, More, Card, and the Falconars, through their writing, helped create a culturally significant political counterpublic.

Gilbert Imlay's "Static Utopia"

Antidemocratic Radicalism

THE 1790S REPRESENT AN EARLY manifestation of what Richard Blaug terms "democratic breakouts," wherein citizens, through participation in a public-sphere community, experience increased political agency.[1] Prominent counterpublics, particularly when organized around important political debates, signal and help foment these breakouts, with late eighteenth-century British abolitionism a redolent example. Anna Laetitia Barbauld's publications reflect the discursive vibrancy of the 1790s. Barbauld tackled political issues such as abolition and education. She also wrote about the public sphere itself. In "Civic Sermons to the People," which Barbauld aptly describes as a "discourse," she urges working-class citizens to reject the popular narrative that it is neither their job nor their right to participate in politics and to resist the cynical argument that if they were to learn about government, that knowledge would inevitably incite disobedience.[2] In this tract, written in response to repressive government sedition laws used to prosecute and jail publishers who printed or distributed radical texts, Barbauld defends free speech and the general public's right to be educated on important social and political issues.[3] She also encourages them to exercise that right. Although she wouldn't have identified it as such, Barbauld was trying to protect what she saw as an essential aspect of democratic governance: the growing and increasingly powerful print public sphere.[4]

Outside explicitly political discourse, popular literature of the period explored these issues in poetry, drama, and novels. Fiction written during the French Revolution that tackled revolutionary polemics generally falls into two scholarly categories: pro-Jacobin or anti-Jacobin. Gilbert Imlay, whose work found a ready audience in 1790s England, took a short-lived but evocative dip into Jacobin literary waters.[5] His two publications, *Topographical Description* and *The Emigrants*, are deeply imbricated in debates about the relationship between politics and private virtue. Although decidedly radical ideas circulate in both books, most prominently arguments in favor of free love and less restrictive divorce laws, they concurrently encourage citizens to focus on individual domestic goals and portray contact with politics—civic engagement— as vitiating. In this way, Imlay's work supports Pocock's argument that belief in civic virtue died with the growth of credit-based capitalism. But books like Imlay's do not represent civic virtue's decline. Instead, they demonstrate the ongoing fear that increased public-sphere participation by the middle classes was dangerous, a reflection of anti-mercantilist sentiments that saw access to luxuries and class competition as a segue to lost virtue—the debate being led by political economists like Smith, Hume, Mandeville, and Shaftesbury. Imlay's books respond to the public-sphere expansion already occurring and they tap into the fears that resulted from this cultural shift. Imlay's work warns against gender perversions driven by greed, reflecting the burgeoning rhetoric of a lost sacred domestic space. While Barbauld applied private morality to public causes and pushed for broader-based participation in politics, demonstrating a commitment to expanding public sphere access, Imlay's seemingly radical work promoted increased separatism and a hardening of the lines between domestic and political life, ultimately negating the democratic import of civic activism.

In *The Emigrants*, the official-sphere institutions of politics, law, and commerce shoulder the blame for domestic vice, with the suggestion that this problem had already reached the urban centers of New England. Instead of promoting a commitment to ethical accountability and social change, Imlay eliminates the specter of moral corruption through a geographic separation between virtuous citizens and the center of official power. Visible in this proposed solution to the threatening degeneration of democratic citizens is what Pocock designated a "static utopia": "The quest for agrarian virtue was the quest for a static utopia, imaginable only as a *rinnovazione*, a renewal of virtue for those who could find lands on which to renew it."[6] Looking toward the future, virtue would fall and the republic with it as soon as there was no more West to settle.

Gilbert Imlay wrote and published during a British civic heyday, a time when revolutionary activity in America and France inspired abundant and active public-sphere debates through which both enfranchised and disenfranchised citizens could offer discursive critiques of the state. Imlay took advantage of this active literary public, creating texts that blend radicalism with a more widely appealing populist message. Imlay turns Rousseau's philosophy into an emigration pitch for the working classes, British subjects who were seeking increased power, not to promote sociopolitical change but to enjoy the economic independence of property ownership.[7] The radical utopia in *The Emigrants* erases the burgeoning civic activism of a lively public sphere by suggesting that the only hope for private virtue and domestic bliss is to create self-governing, separatist, agrarian microcommunities in a new nation, to escape the problems of English politics and start anew. The dominant traits of Bellefont are its location in the West, a nostalgic return to pre-civilized natural gender identities, and a notably homogeneous citizenry. When considered within the debates regarding subaltern citizens' right and ability to participate in the political public sphere, and the relationship between private and public life, Imlay's work is not radical. What it offers is a compensatory and individualistic liberal fantasy that promises dissatisfied white European subjects domestic power and natural virtue through land ownership in the newly minted United States.[8]

Gilbert Imlay's Interesting History

Gilbert Imlay is best remembered as the man who abandoned Mary Wollstonecraft after she gave birth to their daughter, Fanny, out of wedlock, but his work made him a public figure in his own right. *A Topographical Description* was published in England to some acclaim.[9] In it, Imlay details the economic, social, and geographic potential of what was then the West, with a focus on present-day Kentucky. In part because this compendious work was published for a British audience and was an undisguised and impassioned bid for emigration/land purchase, critics have located Imlay's motivation in his checkered financial history. Imlay worked as a land speculator in Kentucky before traveling to Europe. A history of unhappy creditors and legislation against him suggests that his sudden departure from America was not solely for sightseeing or promoting US interests abroad. The portrait of fruitful land and easy opportunity painted by Imlay successfully targeted an audience eager for political change, primed by the American and French Revolutions for the possibility of a more egalitarian nation. Notably, *Topographical Description* influenced Robert Southey and Samuel Taylor Coleridge as they hatched ill-fated plans for a pantisocratic utopia on US soil.[10] It also garnered enough attention to help Imlay find a brief political foothold in France, where he was commissioned to produce papers on the West, further evidence that *Topographical Description* earned Imlay a prominent role in late eighteenth-century transatlantic political discourse.

Because of the heavily political elements in his literature and the various controversies in his life, Imlay's biography is hard to elide. Both his geographic movements and publishing experience seemingly emerged from economic imperatives. Most of the incidents in Imlay's life before he went to Europe are linked to his financial dealings. First, he acted as a government-appointed land speculator, a career that included questionable practices, such as selling land that was already mortgaged. By 1785, when he left America, Imlay had moved about the country to avoid debts and court actions against him. These generally known facts, combined with W. M. Verhoeven's excavation of letters written by Imlay to Silas Talbot, a business partner, convincingly establish the gap between Imlay's actions in his personal life and the political ideals advanced in his published work.[11] After asserting that looser marriage laws would protect women from profligate men, Imlay deserted Mary Wollstonecraft and their daughter for an English actress. The Silas Talbot papers also prove that Imlay, who publicly decried slavery as a political and social ill, was at one time involved in the slave trade. In letters Imlay self-righteously complained of his losses after the ship in which he had a share (the *Industry*) arrived with only half the slaves who began the journey. Imlay did not bemoan the poor conditions that led to so many deaths. He sought to recoup his financial losses. "I have suffered greatly from a variety of circumstances," he lamented. He made his request for a contract dissolution based on "the many disappointments I have sustained."[12] Imlay's concerns were squarely commercial, with no hint of ideological qualms about involvement in the slave trade. Andrew R. Cayton works to counter the common scholarly representation of Imlay as little more than a clever and feckless grifter, arguing instead that Imlay's story helps illuminate an archetype of his time: "Far from a precursor of unscrupulous nineteenth-century capitalists, Imlay was an ambitious young man trying to make his way in a radically unstable revolutionary environment. Economic contraction as well as economic potential defined his world."[13] However, Cayton's own discussion of Imlay's focus on dishonest self-promotion for the sake of personal gain shows that these are not contradictory views. Imlay was both a man of his time and a feckless grifter.

When Imlay moved to England, he left this slave-trading identity behind him. These divergent identities—one revealed by private letters, the other written into his published work—are powerful evidence that Imlay was a master rhetorician who sold a version of himself and of the American West to an interested European audience. Imlay's books should be read as propaganda, influenced significantly in their content by his membership in Jacobin and Girondist circles and his knowledge of contemporary anxieties about mercantilism, classism, and virtue.[14] Imlay's personal history makes his work particularly pertinent for analysis of late eighteenth-century attitudes toward socioeconomic change. His two publications provide a window into both the radical and growing middle-class reading publics of the 1790s and exemplify their desire to learn about other forms of community and governance.[15] They also represent a clear effort to profit from the literary public sphere through targeted appeals. Most scholarly work identifies *The Emigrants* as a Jacobin novel, and certainly Imlay traded in many Jacobin ideas, but his writing was designed to appeal to more than just European dissidents. The private vices in England and the possibility of virtuous renewal in the

United States are reflected in and proffered to a range of middling-class characters.[16] The stars of his novel, the T-n family, whose youngest daughter will "mother" the utopic community of Bellefont into being, are members of the upwardly mobile merchant class. Imlay's writing is one of the earliest examples of the postrevolutionary symbolic capital sought in the imagined America, demonstrating how fluidly these ideas moved between Europe and the United States.[17] In the same years British abolitionist poets warned of Britain's impending corruption at the hand of unchecked greed in the world of trade, Imlay promoted geographic flight from the irredeemable Old World. Abolitionists and other counterpublic activists encouraged increased civic engagement. Imlay promoted an escape from such efforts in the uncorrupted, expansive American West.

A Topographical Description of the Western Territory: Fruitful Land, Domestic Fulfillment

With the exception of Will Verhoeven's comprehensive research, most critics who discuss Imlay's work focus on *The Emigrants* despite its relative obscurity at the time of publication.[18] It is an easy bias to understand after reading both books. *Topographical Description* is disjointed, at times exhaustingly encyclopedic. Imlay inserts long passages written by prominent citizens about America's landscape and commerce, which creates notable inconsistencies in style and content. But for the purpose of understanding Imlay's portrait of America and his vision for a virtuous republican community, it is worth digging into this less accessible, initially more popular book. It lays the groundwork for Bellefont, the static utopia described in *The Emigrants*. The specter of luxury and its capacity to corrupt, fully developed in *The Emigrants*, is quietly present in the underlying economic motivations Imlay offers to encourage the emigration of Britain's middling classes. *Topographical Description* connects liberty to domestic happiness and virtue, erasing the threat of dependency and corruption by suggesting that the US offers unlimited opportunities for agrarian independence. It also exemplifies the contradictions in Imlay's work and life: a vision of western America as a virtue-inducing

Shangri-La that can make land-jobbers like Imlay wealthy through the sale of US land to English investors. The conflict calls attention to the threadbare and unraveling ideological center of Imlay's work and suggests his work was populist salesmanship more than an expression of radical convictions.

In his introduction, Imlay establishes the imagined audience and the purpose of his book. Ostensibly a series of letters written by request to a British friend, its explicit aim is to provide an insider's account of the American West: the rapid growth in population and infrastructure, the beauty and productivity of the land, and the inevitable continuance of growth and prosperity guaranteed by these natural riches. In the first paragraph, Imlay mentions troubles that have overwhelmed continental minds, a sure reference to the political upheavals caused by the French and American Revolutions.[19] While pointing out that an outsider can see things an insider would take for granted, Imlay offers an apology for his critiques of European culture, claiming they are natural offshoots of his personal narrative. "A man who had lived until he was more than five-and-twenty years old, in the back parts of America (which was the case with our author, except during the period he served in the army), accustomed to that simplicity of manners natural to a people in a state of innocence, suddenly arriving in Europe, must have been powerfully stricken with the very great difference between the simplicity of the one, and what is called *etiquette* and good breeding in the other."[20] In reality, Imlay did not live his entire life in the backwoods of America. He lived in Kentucky after the Revolutionary War, but he was born in New Jersey. And it was not a rough and tumble frontier family that molded young Gilbert: "Imlays had married well, produced considerable progeny, accumulated property (including a mill), served as militia officers, and become bulwarks of the local Presbyterian congregation. Growing slowly, New Jersey was a landscape of farms and villages in between the burgeoning metropolises of New York and Philadelphia, both of which beckoned to ambitious young men."[21] To sell the American West to disheartened Englishmen, however, he needed readers to consider the book an authentic account of western life. These lines also establish a rough dichotomy between westerners and Europeans that pervades both of

Imlay's books. Europeans had strayed too far from natural law; their culture now relied on superficial indications of morality, so-called etiquette. The obvious juxtaposition to backwoods Americans' state of innocence is an image of Europe as an overly civilized bed of sin where manners trump morals. Imlay portrays the relationship between English sociopolitical culture and degraded morals more fully in *The Emigrants*, which takes a romantic rather than taxonomic lens to the land and focuses on the corruption of British domestic life.

The introduction to *Topographical Description* begins with idealizing rhetoric about the incipient American empire (i.e., its inevitable growth and moral significance in the Anglo-Atlantic world); it ends with a more practical glorification of the United States. One prominent theme in *Topographical Description* that is more subtly infused into the plot of *The Emigrants* revolves around the economic possibilities inherent in America's natural resources. Imlay begins with a description of the Mississippi River—pointing out the value of its fertile landscape and navigability for traders—and ends by asserting that economic wealth, and more specifically commerce, is the foundation of national strength and stability. Imlay cites empires throughout history that ascended or fell according to their commercial strength. Specifically, he identifies their successful engagement in international trade and the ability to defend maritime rights as the source of imperial power. In the last lines of the introduction, Imlay asserts, "According to the present system, wealth is the source of power; and the attainment of wealth can only be brought about by a wise and happy attention to commerce."[22] Imlay's position reflects the burgeoning rhetoric on commerce discussed in chapter 1, most prominent in the writings of David Hume and Adam Smith. When read against *The Emigrants*, which takes a competing ideological stance by dramatizing the corrupting powers of mercantilism and luxury, holes appear in Imlay's vision of a virtuous, commercially powerful republic. One form of this contradiction materializes in the competing powers Imlay affords land/space in *Topographical Description*. On one hand, he argues that immigrants to the United States can gain liberty and domestic bliss by embracing a purely agrarian existence. Concurrently, on the national level all of this nature (thought of as available land) can provide the US with the commercial productivity and trading power necessary to fortify its borders and protect the lives of the renaturalized men and women who immigrate. But where is the meeting point between a nation that prioritizes international commerce and a solely agrarian citizenry? Imlay attempts to mediate this conflicting vision of public and private national identities in *The Emigrants* through his presentation of a separatist utopia, but the static nature of his imagined community fails to convincingly declaw the threating trajectory of a commercial republic headed toward corruption and decline, a trajectory reinforced by his picture of British society.

In *Topographical Description* Imlay creates a sentimental appeal, which he expands upon in *The Emigrants*, by arguing that the availability of land in America makes marrying and caring for a family economically possible. Imlay extends his audience beyond British radicals, offering an appeal to possible emigrants across socioeconomic classes and political affiliations—to the vast number of British citizens harboring liberal dreams of private property ownership and individual liberty protected by a prosperous republican government.[23] Imlay assures would-be settlers that in the United States, unlike in England, citizens are able to marry young and begin having children not long thereafter. The competition for position and status necessary in England to move one's family forward, according to Imlay, does not exist in America. "No person is jealous of another, because there is room enough for every body. And no man is afraid to marry, because there is a certain obvious resource for maintaining a family comfortably, with moderate industry; and not only so, but also for providing for children, very amply, when they arrive at maturity, arising from the cheapness of land, and the vast produce of the soil."[24] This appeal highlights, with pointed emphasis, the ways in which a citizen's domestic life, economic imperatives, and politics are intertwined. Without suggesting a revolutionary change in the English system, Imlay holds out a promise of increased liberty and economic mobility elsewhere, one that sidesteps the ills of mercantilism. Economic mobility in America can be achieved through idyllic farm life rather than grueling factory work.

He presents land ownership and familial independence as a lofty goal in relatively crowded England. The picture he paints of life in the United States, on the other hand, is intensely romantic. Imlay essentially pledges that for any male English emigrant with basic farming capabilities, two to three years of moderately hard work will yield a farm productive enough to support a family. This promise is an essential component of the United States' power to reconstitute Anglo-Saxon masculinity, a theme that emerges more fully in Imlay's succeeding novelistic portrait of the emasculated Englishman: the availability and fecundity of the land will give Englishmen the independence to control their own lives, reverse the emasculating effects of market competition, and enable swift prosperity in a virtuous home. The expanse of available land also enables the creation of a congenial community by eliminating competition for resources and status. Imlay's image of the US involves a collection of equally independent and agriculturally productive individuals, with no mention of the other roles necessary to produce a commercial trading power. By omitting these merchants and manufacturers from his book, Imlay sidesteps the threats of inequality and dependency.[25] Imlay's utopic agrarianism expunges the anxiety-inducing changes that occurred as labor moved outside the home and offers a nostalgic return to the era before private and political life intersected in their modern forms, before the bourgeois public sphere developed—in other words, feudalistic nostalgia without any compunction regarding the social immobility and inequalities central to this sociopolitical system.[26]

Imlay interweaves descriptions of natural resources in the US with reports on the personalities and lifestyles of settlers. The moral dimension of Imlay's American immigration pitch is exposed in this discussion. At times subtly, at times ham-fistedly, he conflates geographic and agricultural descriptions of the United States with moral gains for the community and the English emigrant. Sugar takes center stage in multiple sections as Imlay seeks to assuage fears that the US cannot provide satisfactory staple goods. Imlay assures prospective immigrants that the ready availability of maple trees in the United States means noninvolvement with the degrading system of slavery needed to extract sugar from the West Indian colonies, an example of how Imlay equates the independence and liberty possible in the US to national virtue, possible only because of abundant natural resources. W. M. Verhoeven identifies this relationship as additional evidence of Jacobin politics. The broad-based civic participation in British abolitionism during this period equally suggests Imlay's ability to read and appeal to bourgeois sociopolitical concerns.[27] Imlay floridly describes a small US sugar-producing settlement consisting largely of soldiers who fought in the Revolutionary War as the (once again, possible) ideal community. These patriots combine an admiration for the arts and other civilizing forces with the social values of backwoodsmen, signifying their uncorrupted tie to nature and the positive natural instincts in man: "Social pleasures were regarded as the most inestimable of human possessions—the genius of friendship appeared to foster the emanations of virtue. . . . Sympathy was regarded as the essence of the human soul, participating of celestial matter, and as a spark engendered to warm our benevolence, and lead to the raptures of love and rational felicity."[28] In Imlay's map of the human soul, connection to the land tethers man to his natural instincts, which are his internal connection to the heavens, a theme that he develops in *The Emigrants*. Imlay loosely and frequently uses terms such as *celestial* and *heavenly* to indicate a character's virtue. By helping men maintain a tie to nature in their daily lives, agricultural work fortifies man's inborn godliness—a natural compass that inspires the community-mindedness and sympathy from which rational felicity springs—and saves him from the dehumanization of mechanized manufacturing work.[29]

He describes a typical day in the settlement, which presages the community of Bellefont created by the hero and heroine in *The Emigrants*. Citizens happily work during the day, while birds fill the air with song. "Enchantment seems to dwell" in the sugar groves where wives and husbands labor side by side. At night everyone in the small community gathers together: "Perhaps a convivial song, or a pleasant narration, closes the scene. Rational pleasures meliorate the soul; and it is by familiarizing man with uncontaminated felicity, that sordid avarice and vicious habits are destroyed."[30] Productive work, a connection to the land, domesticity, and freedom from competition for resources do much more than make citizens independent. These things have the power to eradicate vices that have grown as a result of Europe's overcivilization. In Imlay's books, labor is returned to the home, the government's job is to increase national wealth and therefore power, and the public sphere that helped create Imlay's reading audience seemingly disappears. The great revival of domestic virtue is possible not through the emergence of a renovated republican nation, the education of its growing middle class, or increased participation in democratic governance, but through the return to a social organization that despite the promise of individual property ownership bears a striking resemblance to feudalism, with citizens working the land to produce goods while the national government takes care of broader concerns without civic interference.[31]

THE EMIGRANTS: MERCANTILISM, LUXURY, AND GENDER PERVERSION

The Emigrants reads less as an informational text on the New World than as a fiery representation of the "sordid avarice and vicious habits" of the English.[32] The novel develops Imlay's promise that the United States, and more specifically its broad expanse of unsettled land, offers English men and women the opportunity to reverse the corrupting impact of luxury and overcivilization, in part by suggesting that traveling westward is a way for the British to travel back in time. In an early epistle, Imlay's virtuous heroine Caroline T-n notes: "I have passed from the most populous city in the world—a city embellished with all the beauty that art and ingenuity can furnish, and which the accumulated industry of ages have produced, to the remote corner of the empire of reason and science. But here are charms as well as at masquerades, operas, or the dusty rides in Hyde Park.—Here is a continual feast for the imagination—here every thing is new, and when you contemplate a frowning wilderness, and view the shades or gradations of the polish of manners, which the blandishments of science has produced, and then compare this scene with what must have been the state of Great Britain, and the manners of the Aborigines of that island, when it was first invaded by the more polished Romans, what a comprehensive and sublime subject is it for the human mind?"[33] Caroline's imaginative engagement with wild nature, uninterrupted by masquerades and other civilized entertainments, bonds her to the land. Through immigration to the US, the English can return to their precivilized origins, reconnect with nature, and start anew. The reference to Rome places the United States within the historical narrative of imperial growth and decline. Rome gained polish and then was destroyed by corruption, passing its dominant imperial position to a then-virtuous England that is now destined to follow in Rome's footsteps. Imlay's books present the earliest stage of nation-building as a time when love, sympathy, and virtue were valued above worldly goods. But in his representation of imperial growth and decay as cyclical, and in his failure to present an alternative trajectory, Imlay undercuts the United States' power to meaningfully reconstitute national virtue. This hazy nostalgia also ignores political inequalities that defined classical republics and feudalistic societies. The separatist Bellefont, the novel's solution to domestic corruption within a commercial republic, offers only a romantic return to a mythical premercantile idyll.

The center around which all action and commentary revolves in Imlay's novel is the T-n family. Within their ranks are vicious Englishwomen and Englishmen as well as the brightest ray of hope for America's Anglo-Saxon future, daughter Caroline. Once on American soil, Caroline is reunited with her long-lost uncle, P. P., who fled England with another man's wife. P. P. refused to cow to the unjust laws and social conventions that had exposed his love, Lady B., to the caprices of her debauched husband. He spends the novel teaching Caroline to recognize natural virtue and reject vicious cultural mores. Although characters, in particular P. P., critique English law and government, the more prevalent form of condemnation leveled against England occurs through damning portraits of perversions in gender identity: unfeeling women; cruel, impotent men. Imlay taps into anxiety regarding the spread of luxury in his portrait of a successful mercantile family experiencing unnecessary distress. Luxury's power to corrupt is at the center of all major conflicts and dramatic twists in *The Emigrants*. When the family is introduced, they are struggling financially because of Mrs. T-n's vanity and greed, brought about by an overweening attention to class status. Despite the fact that her husband is a successful merchant, Mrs. T-n develops a colicky response to the merchant class: "The idea of trade shocked her delicacy." To protect her delicacy and increase her social standing, Mrs. T-n insists the family move nearer to court and begins spending money on the luxuries needed to present herself as aristocratic. Her spending, aided and abetted by similar behavior in her son, George, and daughter Mary, drives the family into debt, which in turn forces their emigration. Mr. Il-ray, a friend of the T-n's and a voice of wisdom in the novel, shares this tale with Capt. Arl-ton, a former Revolutionary War soldier destined to fall in love with Caroline. Il-ray describes what particularly troubles him about Mrs. T-n's behaviors: "When I reflect upon the vanity of a woman who regards more the allurements of variety, and the pageantry of fashion, than the future welfare of those beings whom she has brought into the world, my indignation is for a time suspended by my wonder at such unnatural vices."[34] This is one of many passages that demonstrate a set notion of what constitutes natural and unnatural behaviors along gender lines. Here, Mrs. T-n demonstrates a vicious perversion of the natural mothering instinct, a critique heightened by the fact that Mrs. T-n's daughter Caroline is the novel's sympathetic, beleaguered heroine. Il-ray and other characters censure Mrs. T-n's willingness to sacrifice Caroline's future happiness because of selfish, avaricious desires. Despite radical prodivorce rhetoric throughout the novel, the characters and relationships in *The Emigrants* reflect a conventional understanding of feminine virtue as defined by a tender heart and devotion to family, and burgeoning mercantilism is identified as a major threat to those values.

Mary, an apple that did not fall far from the avaricious family tree, poses a different but equally significant threat to her sister Caroline's happiness. And her behavior reinforces Imlay's message that the law and culture of 1790s England erodes private virtues, leading to dishonest, self-interested, and destructive behaviors. Mary plots throughout the novel to keep Caroline and Capt. Arl-ton apart. She deliberately misleads Arl-ton, at one point writing a note she claims is from Caroline. Mary is nonplussed when the stress of these twists and turns makes Caroline faint and fall into a decline—a sign that Caroline has tender sensibilities. When confronted, Mary steadfastly expresses the view that society is simply an aggregate of self-interested individuals. When

Mr. Il-ray engages Mary in a discussion about morality, she laughs at the idea of right and wrong: "Virtue was a word of mere sound, without meaning." Mary is not interested in abstract concepts like virtue and the rights of man, "for it is only realities that give me pleasure and happiness, and every person has a right to obtain them by every means in their power,—and the most adroit and dexterous in saving appearances, appears not only in my eyes, but in the estimation of the world the most meritorious characters."[35] Mary's defense invokes Bernard Mandeville's *Fable of the Bees* and references debates regarding the rights of man in which writers like Edmund Burke, Mary Wollstonecraft, and Thomas Paine were engaged. For a reader considering the disjuncture between the author's private life and his public identity, Mary is a more accurate representative of Imlay than P. P. and Mr. Il-ray, the characters who seem to espouse his political views. Imlay's public persona, in Europe if not in the United States, gained him the reputation of a republican and radical, whereas biographical information reveals he was an expert in profit-driven forms of self-publication.[36] In Mary readers find an individual driven by self-interest and material desires, who attaches merit to public success instead of private (or public) virtues. In the economy of Imlay's novel, Mary's worldview necessitates her eventual expulsion from America and return home to Britain.

Imlay lays the blame for Mary's system of values at the feet of British leaders. The English clergy and government officials, specifically those who maintain power despite whispered knowledge of vicious behaviors, prove that virtue is an irrelevant standard of judgment. If the leaders of the country use "*stratagem, address,* and *corruption*" to maintain power and never think to discuss natural rights, then there is no reason for Mary or other British citizens to contemplate these abstract ideas.[37] Furthermore, Mary contends, if the appearance of greatness rather than virtuous action has maintained the rights of kings, appearances are what actually matter. By using English leaders to defend her own devious and damaging behavior to Caroline, for which she feels neither guilt nor shame, Mary promotes the growing belief that national political and public-sphere ethics deeply inform and impact private virtue. Alongside her mother, Mary shows through her behavior the destruction of women's instinct to love and nurture. Imlay attributes this erosion to political corruption. Instead of protecting citizens from a deluge of morally degrading substance, the government canopy in England has become saturated by immorality: toxic spillover infects vulnerable members of the populace. Mary's rhetoric presages Hannah Arendt's analysis of privacy and publicity in *The Human Condition*, particularly the fear that the social sphere has become so powerful that reputation management supersedes independent self-development in the modern era. This critique of the growing bourgeoisie aligns with Imlay's anti-mercantile message, both of which contribute to the case against an expanding civic body.

In the case of Imlay's English women, national corruption led to an inversion of natural femininity. Women were losing both the instinct to sympathize and the ability to nurture. To show how a corrupt political and social sphere destroys masculinity, Imlay provides readers with a cavalcade of dissipated, impotent Englishmen who instead of protecting women, manipulate and victimize them. Caroline's brother, George, demonstrates the overindulgent, debauched life that young men will lead if brought up in a morally poisoned, luxury-driven environment. Introduced through Capt. Arl-ton's observations, George sleeps in, complains of the rugged travel, and shows absolutely no interest in America's awe-inspiring landscape. These traits stand in direct contrast to Caroline, who walks energetically beside the carriage and devours the scenery while George rides within and bemoans every bump in the road. George cares only for his own material comfort. He is morally and physically weak. Fulfilling the promise inherent in this introduction, George later runs off to the city to gamble away resources the family cannot afford to lose. Mr. Il-ray, once again a critical voice of wisdom, rails against George's selfish behavior: "I am led to believe if such instances of worthlessness are not uncommon, that there must be something radically bad in the present system of morals; for it is impossible for me to believe, that any man can be naturally so unfeeling, as to behold with indifference his family reduced to beggary and wretchedness. . . . Much less to accelerate their inevitable ruin, by a breach of confidence; by a sacrilege against nature and heaven; forgetful of the ties of consanguinity and filial affection—forgetful of the feelings of a man, and the principles of a gentleman. . . . But such are the diabolical effects of those habits, in which many men are educated, and so long accustomed to indulge, that they make every thing, moral, political, and divine, yield to their gratifications."[38] All the terms that define Mary and Mrs. T-n's failures are evident in this strongly worded passage. England's political and social spheres are held accountable for diabolically turning men like George away from virtue, rendering them morally unfit for either domestic or public life. The literal detachment from nature these characters demonstrate reinforces the unnatural quality of English society and values. Ethical corruption at the national level has infiltrated these men's homes and disunited them from nature, heaven, and other people. All that remains in their lives is the pleasure derived from money and material luxuries.

There is hope for George, who is young with an inborn masculine vigor that, through his movement from a life of indolence to one of agrarian labor, will facilitate his reformation. P. P. happily reports in the novel's final letter that George's "understanding has not only been regenerated but his person has already become robust, and he now has more the appearance of an Ancient Briton, than one of those fine fellows, whose nerves require the assistance of harshorn [*sic*], to enable them to encounter the perils of a hackney coach, or the fatigues of a masquerade."[39] Imlay effeminizes British men throughout the novel, and George is saved from a life of feminine fainting spells by his realignment with the precivilized Briton. He recovers the physical strength and manly appearance written into his Anglo-Saxon ancestry, qualities that were lost by the intensely corrupt adult Englishmen in Imlay's novel.[40] Ultimately George is suited, through this transformation, for inclusion in the static agrarian dream. Like Caroline he remains in the United States. Readers are left with the image of a healthy Briton cultivating his farm with wife and children into perpetuity, the horizon line of Imlay's vision for immigrants to the United States. The threat to virtue that adheres to a modern participatory government is no longer a problem when instead one can simply turn back the hands of time and avoid the muddy waters altogether.

Without immigration to America and reeducation at P. P.'s hands, George's future might have been like Lord B's or Mr. F's. It is Mr. F, the husband of Caroline's adored sister Eliza, who provides the most pungent example of emasculating moral corruption. Lord B ruins his wife's reputation by manipulating the rumor-driven social system (spreading lies through the servants and proclaiming the innocent Mrs. B a whore), while Mr. F tries to literally prostitute his wife. After gambling away their wealth, Mr. F offers his wife to a friend for a fee. Once again, readers have Mr. Il-ray's commentary to guide their interpretation of this parable. Beginning with the observation that "the extent and variety of [England's] commerce, has tended to produce an increase of wealth, that is truly wonderful," Il-ray then decries the resultant overindulgence in luxury and the impact of this hyperconsumption on English masculinity. "Effeminacy has triumphed. . . . Nature has its bounds, and vigour is the concomitant of temperance, and exercise, and the charms of fine women can only be relished by men who have not been enervated by luxury and debauchery; and thus it has happened in every populous and wealthy city in the world, that the most lovely women have been neglected by men, whose impotence was as disgusting, as their caprices were unbounded."[41] It is directly stated in this letter that Mr. F is impotent, a charge also leveled against Lord B.[42] These men desire luxury instead of women, and their bodies have been sapped of masculine vigor. The inequality in England's legal system that enables such men to exercise power over their wives, combined with the rampant materialism and social-climbing that Imlay attaches to mercantilism, created physically and morally impotent citizens.

Two male characters exhibit positive natural masculinity and offer a picture of what is possible if faltering Englishmen immigrate to the United States: Caroline's uncle P. P. and her eventual husband, Capt. Arlton. Scholars have discussed Imlay's promotion of a chivalric model of manhood captured by speeches like the one P. P. delivers when budding romance causes Caroline anxiety (note the antiquated syntax and diction): "Tell me all, my charming Caroline, for I am still strong in the feelings of honour; and if aught has been offered to you which is incompatible with your delicacy or sentiments, my feeble arm shall chastise the wretch who has dared to suspect the honour of an insulated and lonely orphan."[43] Chivalric rhetoric, like the feudalistic elements in Imlay's books, suggests that revivifying virtue requires sociocultural regression.[44] Caroline naturally provides the perfect foil for demonstrations of chivalrous action. Corrupt characters are censured for their impact on Caroline. Those who represent natural morality are drawn to her and want to shelter her from harm. The first time they meet, Capt. Arl-ton insists on accompanying Caroline on foot as the family travels through the wilderness, and when she faints at the first sight of Native Americans, Capt. Arl-ton holds her in his arms until she revives.[45] Capt. Arl-ton proves his instinctual understanding of virtue by falling in love with Caroline.

In many ways, *The Emigrants* ends where *Topographical Description* began, by demonstrating how immigration to America can reverse Anglo-Saxon moral decline. Caroline and Capt. Arl-ton marry and found Bellefont, a utopian community in the Ohio Valley. The description of Bellefont's social and political organization is brief and vague. Arl-ton works on the land "with his own hands" every morning and spends the afternoon taking care of business matters; then, in the evening he and Caroline enjoy "the gaiety and festivity of [their] neighbours."[46] Bellefont is a fictionalized version of the purportedly nonfictional sugar-producing community described in *Topographical Description*. In a letter to her sister Eliza, who will soon escape English corruption in order to join them, Caroline describes passing through sugar groves on the way to evening gatherings. This new community was designed and is entirely governed by those who founded it, seemingly with its own laws and culture. What is interesting here is not the brief description provided but the erasures and silences that remain. Class, for one, does not exist in Bellefont because everyone comes from the exact same background. The community is populated by a group of former revolutionary soldiers cast in Capt. Arl-ton's mold. The men cultivate food crops, some of which would necessarily be traded to provide the community with necessities, but no mention is made of interaction with merchants or traders. There are, in this imagined community, no specialized artisans or storekeeping middlemen—only independent farmers. Rosalie

Murphy Baum points out that in a novel committed to the promotion of individual liberty, the lack of individuation in Bellefont is inherently contradictory and even "oppressive."[47] Imlay's choice to suppress all community activities and civic distinctions that could lead to class difference powerfully exemplifies the late eighteenth-century view that corruption of virtue was caused by social mobility and an attendant addiction to luxury. Imlay's static utopia can only survive through a glaring erasure of commerce, class, and racial difference, an erasure that politically serves those in power much more than those seeking to gain it.[48]

Considering *Topographical Description* as a companion piece for *The Emigrants* enables a fuller understanding of the novel's vision of an ideal community. Separation between national power and the domestic sphere constitutes an essential component of Imlay's solution to a dangerous problem: the moral perversions of modern mercantile society. How do individuals avoid the toxic influence of the central government in a nation headed toward imperial status? They form a community that functions independently but recognizes the prosperous federal government as its ultimate source of defense against external threats. In *Topographical Description* Imlay describes the function of a federal government as essentially economic: "The federal government regulating every thing commercial, must be productive of the greatest harmony, so that while we are likely to live in the regions of perpetual peace, our felicity will receive a zest from the activity and variety of our trade." Power derived from trade and control of the seas will give the United States enough international sway to avoid wars or invasions. At the same time it will guarantee the existence of a market for the excess goods produced on small family farms, which will be organized into microcommunities like Bellefont. "Thus in the centre of the earth, governing by the laws of reason and humanity, we seem calculated to become at once the emporium and protectors of the world."[49] The members of Bellefont can toil until 11:00 a.m. and then settle into other business because of the demand that will exist for goods from America. Involvement in agrarian production is represented as unquestionably beneficial to the individual. All of the degraded, vicious English men and women in *The Emigrants* were either aristocrats or merchants, whom Imlay provocatively lumps together. They are alienated from the land and from other people due to the commodity fetishism that instead of being countered by the national government is reinforced by it.

A separatist community can avoid the amoral domesticity caused by corruption within the national government as well as the commercial world. Imlay's vision of the new liberal republic does not venerate the federal government for its ability to integrate the entire community into one brotherhood. He envisions its role as quite the opposite. The federal government's job is to maintain national safety and prosperity while meddling as little as possible in the domestic affairs of its citizens (i.e., laissez-faire government in a liberal society). Communalism on a small scale provides dissatisfied citizens, anxious about the impact of overconsumption and trade on their virtue, with ways to avoid participating in larger, possibly consuming systems of exchange. In order to see Imlay's solution as viable, readers have to avoid gazing too far into the future. Laying aside other impracticalities (a farm that only requires labor between dawn and 11:00 a.m., for example), how will the United States avoid a Roman/English erosion of ethics while fulfilling the promise imagined by Imlay as the next great Empire and "emporium of the world"? If the population grows as a proponent of immigration would certainly desire, the only way for the Bellefonts of America to exist is through a perpetual move westward, or a move in whatever direction allows them semiautonomy from the federal government. A sense of impending doom and antidemocrat sentiment is built into this supposed solution. Imlay's work suggests that contact with the government, even in the mediating realm of civic life, is inevitably corrupting. Seen in this light, instead of offering a beacon of hope for a nation that has recovered early Anglo-Saxon greatness, Imlay's work supports a cyclical and apocalyptic view of mercantilist empires. As wealth and luxuries increase, citizens' private virtue will be corrupted by base pleasure, and this corruption will inevitably sap male citizens of the strength needed to stabilize and defend the republic. In addition to demonizing the economic changes that helped empower England's middle class, this vision renders moot the civic sphere and public activism on the part of citizens.

There is national corruption and private virtue; in *The Emigrants*, no civic activity can stimulate a productive, progressive dialectic between these two bodies. While this novel superficially presents radical Jacobin views, digging beneath the surface exposes an antirevolutionary, regressive, and static heart.

Conclusion

Imlay's bibliography and biography invoke mercantile opportunism more clearly than they promote Jacobinism. These books were Imlay's short-lived effort to capitalize on the growing middle class and the radical reading publics. His attempt to sell land and increase his European trading connections by falsifying his credentials and promoting to working-class and bourgeois citizens a fantasy of agrarian independence. *The Emigrants* foretells both Arendt's and Habermas's fears about transformations in public life, the possibility that in a liberalist society, reputation-management and self-interest will become the public sphere's defining valence. Imlay's work also exemplifies the way in which the public sphere's liberating and subjectifying possibilities have both always been present. While the government was engaged in silencing dissent and public figures like Anna Laetitia Barbauld were fighting for expanded civic discourse, popular literature offered readers an affective entrance into the debate. Imlay's brief writing career occurred amid an immensely vibrant and influential examination of the public sphere itself. As an expert on America and Mary Wollstonecraft's partner, he circulated within socially influential publishing communities that helped shape his work. Seeing Imlay's two books as works of self-promotion—to establish his reputation as an expert and to encourage immigration to the United States based on profit rather than ideals—explains their ideological schizophrenia. Imlay's work does not fit neatly into contemporary or historical categories of radicalism or conservatism. His Rousseauian call for a return to nature, his prodivorce views, and his alignment with Jacobins and Girondists would have earned Imlay the antipathy of conservative British leaders. However, a dramatic return to "natural" forms of gender identity, the homogeneity of his utopic community, and his promotion of political noninvolvement by these communities are ultimately antidemocratic. Wanting to return to a primitive, semifeudal sociopolitical state appeals to those seeking political escapism: the separatist agrarian fantasy offers flight from the complications, challenges, and battles of citizenship in a participatory democracy. It also erases questions of power, exactly the kind of questions being asked by visible and influential counterpublics throughout the 1790s.

THE VIRTUE OF SELF-GOVERNMENT

Fear of, or Faith in, the People

IN *THE AMERICAN DEMOCRAT* JAMES Fenimore Cooper laments changes in US culture just fifty years after independence. He rails against an overly influential and pandering press, the failure of Americans to appreciate social etiquette and propriety, and the growth of demagoguery. All of these issues are linked to Cooper's belief that the greatest threat to a democratic republic is the demos itself. In Cooper's eyes, the practical guard against such threats to sociopolitical stability is private property. "Property is desirable as the ground work of moral independence, as a means of improving the faculties, and of doing good to others, and as the agent in all that distinguishes the civilized man from the savage."[1] In this passage, Cooper echoes Aristotelian notions of citizenship and civic virtue. The property owner alone is fit to participate in civilization; all others carry with them the taint and threat of savagery, which suggests an inability to think rationally or to understand abstract political ideals.[2] Those who do not own property cannot be trusted to develop a stable, independent, moral self; they are followers who must be led. When *The American Democrat* was published, the property-owning class was relatively monolithic. Cooper's idea of what's required to attain moral independence denies that capacity to women, slaves, and the poor. In this chapter I focus on how two historical romance novels, Cooper's *The Spy* and Catharine Maria Sedgwick's *The Linwoods*, offer competing visions of civic virtue that carry with them broader implications about who should or should not play a role in shaping the nation's culture and politics.[3] These two novels, by diverging in their representation of the individual capacity for self-government and moral growth, promote disparate visions of democracy and republicanism. Cooper warns against allowing members of the demos a political voice. Sedgwick suggests the promise of an expanded political public sphere and increased participation across identity groups.

Scholars continue to debate the political anxieties and attitudes that dominated early American literature. Americanists have challenged the longstanding presumption that this period was marked by an unadulterated celebration of liberal values, in particular private property's role in creating a stable community and complacent representations of America as a classless society. Gerald J. Kennedy shows the extent to which literary nationalism "unfolded in a social milieu of class and ideological conflict precipitated by the economics of the market revolution." Joe Shapiro argues that one need not look far to find nineteenth-century American fiction that "reveal[s] members of the U.S. bourgeoisie to be in fact deeply anxious about their participation in market relations, and about the consequences for themselves of economic individualism and market-based competition."[4] Nowhere is this clearer than in historical fiction like Cooper's and Sedgwick's. Both return to the revolutionary era, but with a keen interest in the ongoing relationships between economics, politics, and republican virtue. The war provides an opportune setting for exploring national self-conceptions and for mythologizing the ideal citizen. Characterizing these works as liberal or illiberal is not my goal, but the issues that emerge in discussion of liberalism—individualism, private property, and class mobility—deeply inform their representation of virtuous citizenship.

In *The Spy* republican civic virtue can only be achieved and maintained by those already in power, and their power and property are constantly under threat from overreaching political subalterns. White propertied men demonstrate virtue through active leadership and a willingness to sacrifice their lives for the nation, displaying the classical masculine form of virtù that was being challenged in eighteenth-century British discourse, which praised middle-class domestic (often feminized) notions of virtue. Arguably in response to this sea change, Cooper works to recodify civic leadership as the sole province of an American aristocracy. Women, black Americans, and lower-class characters in *The Spy* are portrayed as virtuous only if they subjugate themselves to a narrowly defined leading class. Because these populations cannot be trusted to temper passions with reason—essential for self-governance—their actions, and by extension their relationship to public life, must be mediated by white patriarchs. This belief finds expression in *The Spy* through Cooper's negative portrayal of mobility in all its guises: physical, social, and economic. It also emerges in his representation of romantic and familial relationships. Shirley Samuels delves into the links between individual, family, and nation in early American literature: "The reciprocal work of the family . . . seems to be to create selves who create families who create states in the image of the family."[5] Samuels's words capture the cyclical nature of this narrative trope as well as the flexible and variant depictions of influence between private and public identities. In this vein, Cooper suggests that stability in the nation requires stability in domestic relations, and roles within the home and within the public sphere must be aligned for all citizens. In this story of US origins, the growing civic identity that diffused discursive power and offered political agency to disenfranchised citizens is expunged. Both *The Spy* and *The American Democrat* relegate political subalterns to a wholly private identity within the nation.

Sedgwick challenges Cooper's ideological foundations through the tale of Isabella Linwood's personal and political development. Isabella demonstrates the intellectual abilities that represent in Sedgwick's novel the most essential components of virtuous republican citizenship: rational deliberation and self-governance. By disentangling property ownership from the ability to form "moral independence," Sedgwick's novel challenges the dominant national narrative, which sought to create "a fabulous origin" that reified privacy and private property. As Elizabeth Maddock Dillon argues, "In narrative terms, private property thus stands as the origin of liberal autonomy: property ownership enables one to move forward into the public sphere." This standard for public-sphere participation helps maintain the white, patriarchal power structure. White males own private property; "white women and blacks [are represented] as producers and species of property."[6] In *The Linwoods*, limitations on property ownership are obviously in place, but property is stripped of its moral significance. Instead, Sedgwick glorifies intellectual mobility and a healthy middle class. Isabella Linwood overcomes her aristocratic background, evident in unkind and imperious youthful behavior, by developing a rational appreciation for democratic principles, a change requiring deliberation and autonomous self-construction. There are echoes of Adam Smith's *Theory of Moral Sentiments* in Sedgwick's portrait of Isabella as a model of virtuous republicanism. In addition to promoting the domestic virtues, Smith elevated self-denial and self-government above the rest, arguing that without self-governance people are unable to consistently practice all other virtues.[7] Defining republican virtue as an intellectual capacity not tethered to gender, class, or racial identities creates a civic space that is open to anyone capable of self-government. While Sedgwick's promotion of this space does not explicitly challenge political inequality, it makes civic identity available to marginalized citizens, creating the possibility for sociopolitical transformation from the margins.

The American Democrat: Containing the Demos

Including the term *aristocratic* in a description of Cooper's politics is not without controversy. Scholars have long debated Cooper's ideological perspective, specifically his attitude toward democracy, republicanism, and aristocracy. There's good reason for this debate. As Heinz Ickstadt points out, Cooper "rarely made use of the dominant political rhetoric of the period which set the People (the mass of honest producers) against the Aristocrats (the moneyed and idle few)."[8] Cooper formulated his own view of a growing aristocracy in America, one constituted by increasingly wealthy and politically influential businessmen. Allan M. Axelrad takes issue with the loose application of the term *aristocratic* in Cooper studies and points out that Cooper "clung to an idealized vision of an eighteenth-century New York that was led by rural gentry motivated by noblesse oblige."[9] The phrase noblesse oblige conjures romantic notions of hereditary aristocracy, a system in which political leadership and cultural power sat largely in the hands of those born into aristocratic privilege. I agree with Axelrad on this point. Cooper's writing celebrates a hierarchical relationship between well-bred gentlemen and political subalterns, which is one reason Cooper's position is patently proaristocracy.

Axelrad argues that Cooper regularly used the term *aristocracy* to describe a growing oligarchy. John P. McWilliams and Dorothy Waples accept the more common conception of aristocracy but suggest an Americanization of the idea in Cooper's work. McWilliams argues that "if Cooper has an aristocratic bias, it is a bias toward Jeffersonian natural aristocracy and not toward Adam's longings for distinctions of title." Waples claims that he "believed in such a thing as personal aristocracy without political aristocracy."[10] It is true that Cooper's antimonarchy rhetoric eschews the value of titles and that much of his work focuses on glorification of the role played by educated gentlemen rather than inherited political power. But there are significant unmined implications in this conception. If the natural aristocracy includes only white property-owning males, Cooper's concept of natural hierarchy is built on heredity—not only on racial heredity but also on inherited wealth. Early American works often vaunted economic mobility and the absence of classism, which as Joseph Shapiro points out can be traced to De Crevecoeur and other popular presentations of Jeffersonian democracy. It is important to note that "those who were forced to sell their labor power in order to survive in the early United States more often than not barely eked out their subsistence, and rarely did they accumulate wealth enough to become buyers of labor or to permit their children to become buyers of labor."[11] Although Cooper's self-representation reflects early nineteenth-century notions of relative political meritocracy, this perspective was predicated upon class, race, and gender hierarchies. There is no simple divide between personal and political aristocracy. Hierarchies in personal relationships were codified into laws that limited voting rights and property ownership, and in the case of slaves a denial of the most basic human rights.

The American Democrat

Cooper approaches the issue of hierarchy and social mobility from multiple angles. For literary scholars, one of the most interesting aspects of

The American Democrat is Cooper's discussion of language and popular journalism, which foregrounds the print public sphere. He presents the press as a corrupt source of sociopolitical influence and a major contributor to the dangerous democratization of society. This view seeps through in Cooper's critique of newspapers and his protracted attention to language. The book nostalgically contrasts the Revolutionary War–era press with its contemporary incarnation: "In America, while the contest was for great principles, the press aided in elevating the common character, in improving the common mind, and in maintaining the common interests; but, since the contest has ceased, and the struggle has become one purely of selfishness and personal interests, it is employed, as a whole, in fast undermining its own work, and in preparing the nation for some terrible reverses."[12] Cooper accuses the press not just of reflecting corrupt politics but of playing a role in the devolution of American culture. In England, Cooper argues, the great men are more geographically concentrated and can exercise a greater influence on the press (and the general public). In the US these few exceptional men are spread around the country, allowing the common man a dangerous level of influence on American newspapers, which by pandering to a self-interested popular audience accelerate the nation's decline.

Cooper accuses newspapers and politicians of manipulating language to gain influence over this irrational and therefore easily manipulated population. To flatter their pride and appeal to the competitive self-interest of readers, journalists and politicians call laborers "gentlemen" and gentlemen "folks." Cooper devotes a section of *The American Democrat* to language because he believes such slippages and shifting attitudes toward words that indicate social station reflect a larger problem: the troubling fluidity of private and public relationships. Cooper fears growing resistance to the terms *servant* and *master*, which he sees as accurate and valuable delineations of hierarchy, and bemoans the increasing misapplication of the word *gentleman* to merchants and other working-class men, which strips it of meaning. A gentleman, in Cooper's eyes, is a man born into enough wealth to devote much of his life to cultural education. He owns property and has a sophisticated understanding of politics, history, and the arts. He is essentially an American aristocrat who through his wealth and position is capable of classical republican freedom and intellectual autonomy. The public-sphere discursive diminution of the terms *gentleman* and *master* is a challenge to the framework upon which social order delicately rests. These slippages represent a threat to the kind of autonomy that relies upon the labor of others in a patriarchal home, namely the relative freedom from necessity that a person in Cooper's position might enjoy.

Cooper's anxious attention to discourse comes to a head in his discussion of the phrase We the People, a lightning rod for proegalitarian public-sphere rhetoric. The essential problem is that the general populace twists these words for personal gain. Demagogues use the phrase to appeal to constituents, promising them an increased equality that is impossible and entirely undesirable. This overglorification of equality distorts the intentions of the US Constitution and encourages a sociopolitically dangerous expansion of democracy. As evidence, Cooper points out that women were not intended to participate in the governing process.[13] According to Cooper, We the People applies solely to elected representatives. And where the equality of rights is concerned, "it has been carried as far as prudent discretion will at all allow. . . . Equality is no where laid down as a governing principle of the institutions of the United States."[14] Extending the vote to women and others who do not own property threatens to further damage the moral, cultural, and political tenor of the United States.

Cooper's overarching argument is that in a democracy, individual Americans must guard against the masses rather than powerful leaders. This presumption informs Cooper's contention that democracy must be severely limited and balanced by the maintenance of existing hierarchies, personal and political. His view of Congress reinforces his message: "Congress is composed of many, while the executive is one, bodies of men notoriously acting with less personal responsibilities than individuals. . . . It follows that the legislature of this country, by the intention of the constitution, wields the highest authority under the least responsibility, and that it is the power most to be distrusted." Cooper's belief that broader participation in governance equates to less moral autonomy and virtue is fundamentally antidemocratic and informs his attitude toward the People, whose influence on Congress he virulently fears: "The public, every where, is proverbially soulless. All feel when its rights, assumed or real, are invaded, but none feel its responsibilities."[15] Cooper's allegiance and trust lie at the top of the hierarchy, and from various angles he urges patriotic leaders to constrain the threat of broadening political participation by a soulless public, down to the policing of idiomatic changes to language denoting social station. In his critiques of language and of the press, he betrays his belief that public discourse is both an indicator and source of social change. Stemming the dangerous tide of democratization means, in part, denying America's political underclasses the opportunity to participate in public discourse and doing everything possible to undercut their credibility as the political public sphere expands.

THE SPY: PROTECTING THE NATION FROM TRANSGRESSIVE PRIVATE CITIZENS

Cooper lays out much of his political philosophy in *The American Democrat*. But it is in his fiction that these positions come to life. *The Spy* exemplifies conservative ideology and the ability of fiction to illuminate politics: "Behind the riot in the street or debate in Parliament is the maid talking back to her mistress, the worker disobeying her boss. That is why our political arguments . . . can be so explosive: they touch upon the most personal relations of power. It is also why it has often fallen to our novelists to explain to us our politics."[16] *The Spy* offers a fictionalized solution to what Cooper sees as the danger of democratization. While the American Revolution may have necessitated a transgression of social boundaries, Cooper makes no space in the postwar nation for public recognition of politically marginalized citizens. Republican virtue and national stability depend upon political subaltern's tethering to property-owning men, whose intellect and economic autonomy fit them for leadership in the home and the nation.[17]

The plot revolves around two axes. First is the Wharton family's saga. Mr. Wharton moves his two daughters and spinster sister-in-law from New York City to the neutral ground of Westchester as a protective maneuver, hoping to avoid direct conflict and protect their remaining property. Sarah, the elder Wharton daughter, loves a redcoat, Captain Wellmere, and espouses loyalist sentiments. Her sister, Frances, is devoted to the revolutionary cause and to the Virginian Peyton Dunwoodie, a major in the Continental army. The novel opens with the clandestine visit of Sarah and Frances's brother, Henry, a valorous British soldier whose capture, trial, and escape serve as a locus for conflicts and connections between the various characters. As these familial scenes unfold, the reader follows the movements of Cooper's titular spy, Harvey Birch. A lowly peddler believed by other characters to be devoted only to financial gain, Birch uses this cover and the mobility of his lifestyle to act as an influential American spy, answering directly to George Washington. The Cowboys and the Skinners, groups of villainous thieves, play an equally important role in the novel and represent an inverted image of Harvey Birch. Birch uses his reputation for greed to cover up patriotic acts; the Skinners pretend to act in the name of patriotism solely for personal gain. *The Spy*'s multiple plot lines invoke the power and danger of false appearances while valorizing those who understand their social identity and fulfill their roles properly.

The Spy attempts to prove the need for civil restraints and for a population of men (and women) who accept their subordination—at home and in public—rather than pursuing increased sociopolitical power. Almost all the novel's central characters, at one point or another, appear in disguise. The people dramatically fail to present an exterior self that is stable and easily identifiable, emphasizing Cooper's anxiety regarding unfixed, mobile social identities. Some literally disguise themselves while others mask their true intentions, beliefs, or war-related activities. Henry Wharton wears a disguise to reach his family homestead; Harvey Birch disguises himself as Betty, the camp mother, and later as a preacher; and the family slave Caesar dresses as Henry to assist in his escape from prison. Even George Washington, the father of the republic, appears in two distinct forms: the upstanding father of the nation and a disguised spy (Harper) traversing the neutral ground to procure information. More subtle and sometimes insidious examples of masking (no physical disguise is worn but motives and ideals are purposely hidden) include

Colonel Wellmere's hidden English marriage and the falsely proclaimed patriotism of the Cowboys and Skinners. Emily Budick argues that "for Cooper, the unnatural state of war is also the natural state of existence. Disguise is a condition of reality; concealment, a fact of life."[18] In *The American Democrat* Cooper attaches this reality not just to war but also to democratic developments in the postrevolutionary republic. Characters in *The Spy* who have no place in the postwar United States are those who transgress their socially determined positions: servants who resent their duties, women who seek to lead rather than follow, and lower-class citizens who loot private property to gain wealth and power.

The most explicitly malevolent characters in *The Spy* are the Cowboys and the Skinners, marauding bands of thieves who mask their motives behind political affiliations. Although on the surface lower-class characters in this novel "mainly add comic effect and perform necessary plot functions," scenes featuring the Cowboys and the Skinners are politically significant.[19] If these men are taken to represent a sampling of the American masses, then fraternal affection cannot reliably bond together and stabilize the national community, thus the need for clear hierarchies and powerful leadership in both the individual and national family. Historically, the Cowboys were men loyal to the British cause; the Skinners claimed revolutionary sympathies. In Cooper's novel, however, neither group cares about political or social causes. Each individual seeks only to increase his own wealth, and the allegiances they create with one another exist solely to augment plunder. One man does not hesitate to offer up his brother's whereabouts to save his own neck. In addition to critiquing the greed of lower-class citizens, Cooper echoes the treasonous Andre/Arnold affair by presenting a traitorous brother and the eventual hanging of a Skinner. In *Notions of the Americans*, Cooper addressed the Andre/Arnold affair directly: "Among men of high and honourable minds, there can be but one opinion concerning this enterprise. There is something so repugnant to every loyal sentiment in treason, that he who is content to connect himself, ever so remotely, with its business, cannot expect to escape altogether from its odium."[20] In *The Spy* treachery among the lower classes is odious whereas upper-class men who engage in subterfuge (including George Washington) appear purposeful, devoted, and admirable. (Harvey Birch, the titular spy, is a complicated exception whom I discuss later.)

One of the novel's principal concerns is what will happen to the nation if the Skinners, or men like them, obtain positions of power solely through an increase in wealth. The implication is that if men are rewarded for the accumulation of wealth alone—addressed and treated like gentlemen simply because of their economic status—the basest and most rapacious might rise to power. Before punishing the Skinners with his whip, the valorous, virtuous, and wellborn Captain Lawton mockingly assures their leader that he will find his due reward when the war is over: "Press the point of your own services, and rail at the Tories, and I'll bet my spurs against a rusty nail that you get to be a county clerk at least." With less irony the unethical Captain Wellmere assures the Skinners, following a raid, "There is plate and money enough to make you all gentlemen."[21] Cooper's disapproval of social mobility in *The American Democrat* and his caution against the loose usage of the term *gentleman* appear here in fictional form. Lawton's and Wellmere's speeches, taken together, signal the possibility of a savage populace purchasing political and cultural power. The Skinners represent the most extreme version of man as driven only by self-interest. The implied threat is that if democratization is pushed too far, men like these could one day be leading the country.

The Skinners and the Cowboys, a dramatic representation of the threatening masses, live at one extreme of human nature and are portrayed as animalistic. The warning inherent in their depiction is fortified and extended to the middling classes by Cooper's portrait of rebel soldiers. In scenes featuring field soldiers and their superiors, the need for *aristocratic* leaders most clearly emerges. Despite fighting on the right side of the war, actuated by patriotism, the cavalry soldiers are untrustworthy and irrational. When faced with danger, the undifferentiated dragoons fail to maintain their virtuous civic commitments. Conversely, the actions of Maj. Peyton Dunwoodie and Captain Lawton demonstrate the capacity of extraordinary men, who happen to be of aristocratic lineage, to control and properly channel the soldiers' passion. Twice in the novel the American troops succumb to fear and fall into chaos or retreat.

The first time, Major Dunwoodie swiftly regains control: "Riding between this squadron and the enemy, in a voice that reached the hearts of his dragoons, he recalled them to their duty. His presence and words acted like magic. The clamour of voices ceased; the line was formed promptly and with exactitude; the charge sounded; and, led on by their commander, the Virginians swept across the plain with an impetuosity that nothing could withstand." Dunwoodie's leadership skills are nearly mythical as he demonstrates the power of a true gentleman to positively influence the men around him. He harnesses the emotional energy of an impetuous mass through the sheer force of his presence and voice, a task Lawton will repeat in the final battle scene. Before charging into the fight that ends his life, Lawton uses "all the strength of his powerful voice" to remind the troops of their duty, until "they demanded to be led against their foe once more."[22] Cooper's language in this scene shows that the troops did not imbibe their leaders' strength and take to battle as self-controlled individuals. After recalling their patriotic emotions, they were roused again to follow a compelling leader, a man who knows how to use his voice. Over the course of the novel, the general populace of cavalrymen grow no steadier nor more trustworthy in the discharge of their duties. Though their patriotism lends moral purpose to their passions, they remain fundamentally irrational and impetuous like their more sinister counterparts, the Skinners. These scenes suggest that the American Revolution was won less by the people than by the exalted men who led them, a representation designed to tamper claims that the United States' violent birth and the antityranny rhetoric that played such a prominent role in revolutionary writings should be applied to postwar nationalism. As Cooper argues in *The American Democrat*, equality and democracy had been stretched far enough. Any further, he suggests in *The Spy*, and the country will become a chaotic, rudderless nation, ripe for demagoguery.

The troops' behavior in battle scenes and at rest provides a microcosm of Cooper's solution to the threat of political instability. Recognizing and following powerful leaders is one piece of the puzzle; another piece is revealed in the military leaders' fervent wartime commitment to mealtime etiquette. Cooper's dinner scene in the midst of war emphasizes the political implications of domestic relations. Who enters first, where they sit, how and by whom the table is set all signal the relative power of community members, as when Dunwoodie, Frances, and those closest to them share a meal: "In taking their places at the board, the strictest attention was paid to precedency; for, notwithstanding the freedom of manners which prevailed in the corps, points of military etiquette were at all times observed, with something approaching to religious veneration." Despite the chaos and depredations of war, Dunwoodie, Lawton, and the Whartons enjoy a well-served and socially proper meal at camp. The narrator describes the attire of men and women, the order and style in which they enter the dining room, and the dishes themselves. The Whartons' black servant Caesar, who is lauded throughout the novel for understanding his position and respecting convention, jealously guards the table he has set and stands tensely until they are all "comfortably arranged around the table, with proper attention to all points of etiquette and precedence. The black well knew the viands were not improving; and though abundantly able to comprehend the disadvantage of eating a cold dinner, it greatly exceeded his powers of philosophy to weigh all the latent consequences to society which depend on social order."[23] The narrator's commentary infantilizes Caesar while portraying him as a model of servitude. Though he does not have the rational capacity to understand the significance of specific social conventions, he is happy to mimic these conventions because they were mandated by the men nature carved out to lead him. Through his performance of childlike deference to a patriarchal leader, Caesar properly reflects his subjugated status within the nation and earns the approval of the heroic protagonists.

The essential role played by proper deference is explicitly defined in *The American Democrat*. Cooper describes an old woman whose family members care for her when she is too old to work. They fulfill their role as masters as faithfully as she fulfilled hers as a servant. She understood that "they who serve owe a respectful and decorous obedience, showing by their manner as well by their acts, they understand that without order and deference, the different social relations can never be suitably filled." In *The Spy* Cooper laments the diminution of such men as Caesar: "The face of blacks of which Caesar was a favourable specimen is becoming very rare. The old family servant, who, born and reared in the dwelling of his master, identified himself with the welfare of those whom it was his lot to serve, is giving place in every direction to that vagrant class which has sprung up within the last thirty years, and whose members roam through the country unfettered by principles, and uninfluenced by attachments."[24] The threat of mobility is polyvalent: physical mobility and lack of attachment to a home/property are associated with the loss of a moral center, and individuals who unmoor themselves become ethically unfettered. Cooper's rhetoric about mobility, property, and attachment throughout the book shows the extent to which a conception of civic identity that centers around property can be used to rationalize the need for subjugation of disenfranchised citizens. Caesar could not have owned property in the eighteenth century; neither could the female characters in this novel. To avoid becoming dangerous vagrants, they must remain connected and subservient to a patriarchal property owner.

The romance at the center of Cooper's novel exemplifies proper domestic and political subordination. Frances Wharton, the feminine ideal, is beautiful, innocent, and aristocratic. She joyfully subjugates herself to Dunwoodie and other exceptional men. Although Frances shows heroic qualities when she scales a mountain to rescue her brother, the scene ends with her seeking and receiving benediction from Harper/George Washington: "A tear was glistening on either cheek, and her mild blue eyes were gazing upon him in reverence. Harper bent and pressed a paternal kiss upon her forehead." Images of Frances giggling, crying, and acknowledging her own weaknesses as a woman throughout the novel demonstrate the need for patriarchal care. The first time Frances and Dunwoodie interact provides an accurate and telling schematic of her identity and their relationship: "Her eyes spoke volumes, but her tongue was silent;—her hands were interlocked before her, and, aided by her taper form, bending forward in an attitude of expectation, gave a loveliness and an interest to her appearance." Frances's physical position in this scene is one of supplication, and she literally has no voice. Throughout the novel she is described as kneeling in front of influential male characters, most significantly the forthcoming leaders of the new republic, Captain Dunwoodie and Harper/Washington. These private moments parallel Frances's political identity. When Henry Wharton claims that "women are but mirrors, which reflect the images before them," Frances acquiesces. "I must confess I am indebted to the Major for my reasoning." Like Caesar, Frances herself cannot reason, so she relies on Dunwoodie as an intermediary and interpreter of national politics: those who cannot reason must remain politically subjugated. Elizabeth Maddock Dillon observes, "Because women's bodies have been seen to constrain and encumber them, women have been understood to lack the constitutive agency that would enable them to participate in liberal subjectivity. . . . The logic of this particularization of women involves not simply pulling rank—arguing that men are more authoritative, muscular, rational, or closer to God than women—rather, it requires defining women as individuals constitutively unable to exercise choice and agency."[25] While much of the scholarship on sensibility deals primarily with gender, Caesar's representation reflects the common application of this trope to nonwhite characters as well. Women and African Americans are constrained by their natural weaknesses and must be denied agency to maintain a stable national community.

Cooper accentuates the propriety of Frances's obedient deportment by including a feminine foil, Isabella Singleton, who is also in love with Peyton Dunwoodie. Through Isabella's and Harvey Birch's stories, Cooper works to cypher the revolutionary element out of the revolution, making it clear that role transgression has no place in the postwar United States.[26] Isabella is the dark to Frances's light. Her black hair and eyes contrast with Frances's blonde, blue-eyed, pale beauty, as her fiery nature highlights Frances's quiet pliability. The narrator describes Isabella as "wild," "enthusiastic," and "changeable"; after forcefully "conquering the violence of her feelings," she apologizes to Frances for her "ungovernable feelings." Isabella, incapable of sustained rationality, fails to subsume her passions and follow the leader. As Isabella is dying, she offers Frances a benediction, acknowledging the unseemliness of intense and uncontrolled passion in a woman. This soliloquy and Dunwoodie's reassurance comfort the unassuming Frances, who doubted her own value. "'Lovely enthusiast!' cried Dunwoodie, 'you know not yourself, nor me. It is a woman, mild, gentle, and dependent as yourself, that my very nature loves.'"[27] Neither woman is able to govern her own emotions. Frances's virtue lies in accepting her failure as a natural feminine weakness. Both Isabella's expressions of regret and her fate—she dies single and childless when a stray bullet enters the cabin—solidify Cooper's message. She was a hero of the Revolution but she is neither a true national ancestor nor a model for postwar republican womanhood.

Harvey Birch, the titular spy, presents readers with a representation of lower-class citizens, analogous in multiple ways to Isabella Singleton's transgressive femininity. Early critics of *The Spy* worked to identify a real-life inspiration for Birch, who has intrigued and troubled scholars for decades. Later critics focus on the political dimensions of a heroic character who exemplifies the mobility and perfidy that Cooper seemingly censures.[28] Harvey and Isabella are sympathetic and self-sacrificing characters, roused to heroics by their patriotism. They both step outside their proper roles from a passionate desire to aid the revolutionary cause, and both ultimately acknowledge that their nonconformity renders them unfit for domestic and public life. When Washington lauds Harvey at the end of his service by proclaiming him "one of the very few that I have employed who have acted faithfully to our cause. . . . To me, and to me only of all the world, you seem to have acted with a strong attachment to the liberties of America," Harvey raises his flushed face "proudly swelling with his emotions, but with eyes that modestly sought the feet of the speaker."[29] This scene offers a key to the seeming contradiction in underclass heroism. Harvey stands in relation to Washington much as Frances posed in front of Dunwoodie: eyes cast downward, modesty intact. He accepts subjugation, silence, and anonymity. When Washington writes Harvey a note that will assure future descendants he was a patriot, Harvey protests—how can he have children when they would suffer from the infamy attached to his name? Instead, Harvey remains a solitary wanderer, never truly at home in the nation.

The presence of Isabella Singleton and Harvey Birch in Cooper's tale, despite their clear moral motivation and the positive roles they played in achieving America's independence, does not mitigate the threat of social mobility represented by the Skinners. In fact, their inclusion strengthens the message that recognition of social distinctions and respect for systems of hierarchy are central to domestic and national stability. Through these characters Cooper offers a vision of republicanism that is considerably more aristocratic than democratic. Yes, these individuals are heroic and should be appreciated, but their actions have value only in the extremity of war. If Americans want a virtuous postwar republic, they must fulfill the roles they inherit, as Frances and Caesar so readily do. Attempting to subvert these roles, which exist to provide guidance for those who are incapable of rational self-governance, will lead to a country of dangerously untethered individuals. As the Skinners demonstrate, this unmooring can result in lost principles and greed-driven attempts to wrest political and social power from those who should lead. Private citizens (i.e., nonwhite, nonmale, non-property-owning) must remain bound to their white, male, aristocratic guides who can protect them from the dangers of public life, and protect the nation from them.

The Linwoods: Self-Governance, Private Virtue, and Public Voices

The Linwoods, written fourteen years after *The Spy*, mines the same genre conventions to offer readers a distinct national origin story. The essential components of Cooper's democratic vision—distrust of disenfranchised citizens, fear of social and political mobility, and reverence of aristocracy—become more starkly evident when read alongside *The Linwoods*. Sedgwick's and Cooper's work has been discussed in tandem by a number of scholars, with gender a logical through line of comparative analyses. Although their frontier novels receive significantly more attention than those set during the revolution, the political distinctions and dynamics identified in their thematically paired texts tend to reflect the consistency of Sedgwick's and Cooper's respective ideological positions. Carolyn L. Karcher encourages readers to recognize that "the two authors' revisions of each other's plots reflect more than literary rivalry. . . . At stake in their jousting is whether patriarchal or protofeminsit ideology will shape the frontier romance and the vision of American history it encodes."[30] As Nina Baym argues, women's historical writing is often revisionist without being radical.[31] While this pattern applies to

The Linwoods on multiple levels, there are radical implications in challenging a patriarchal stranglehold on civic identity. A fiery, dark-haired Isabella (the center of the tale) becomes an icon of republican womanhood rather than the subject of a cautionary tale of unregulated, self-destructive female passion. Sedgwick's Isabella does not partner with a southern-plantation-owning military hero. She rejects an aristocratic suitor to marry a New England farmer's son. These differences reflect two of *The Linwoods'* central messages: virtue and sociopolitical stability flourish in the middling classes (versus a New World aristocracy), and white propertied men are not the only citizens capable of rational self-governance and moral autonomy.

Much of Sedgwick's politics emerge through the novel's romantic and domestic relationships. Narrative commentary urges movement away from aristocratic values in domestic life while celebrating middle-class virtue. On the final page, Sedgwick inserts a didactic critique of the aristocracy's cultural influence, specifically holding "the growing imitation of the artificial and vicious society of Europe" responsible for mercenary marriages and the un-American values such unions represent. Sedgwick's advice to readers foretells the stance she later takes in her autobiography: a middle-class life is the best guarantor of virtue.[32] Sedgwick also critiques Federalists, like her father, who stood "with their feet firmly planted on the rock of Aristocracy" and attributes their "thorough distrust of 'the people'" to lingering monarchical values. Sedgwick's female readers are urged to "imitate our heroine in trusting to the honourable resources of virtue and talent, and a joint stock of industry and frugality, in a country that is sure to smile upon these qualities, and reward them with as much worldly prosperity as is necessary to happiness, and safe for virtue."[33] Sedgwick's advice promotes Adam Smith's privately oriented virtues of "frugality and industry," and her warning recalls the discourse on liberty versus dependency. Sedgwick argues that poverty and the worldly life of an aristocrat render people dependent upon others, whether by charity or social approval, thus limiting their autonomy. Those who demonstrate privately oriented middle-class virtues are able to exercise rational self-governance, making them capable of a stable civic subjectivity, while aristocratic characters are portrayed as dependent and morally inconstant.

Sedgwick suggests a correlation between aristocratic values and patriarchal domestic relations that diminish the individual capacity for self-governance. Relationships that require obedience on one side and dominance on the other damage the ability of both members to make rational and moral judgments. Isabella's parents, in particular, serve as a warning against the ethical degradation when a patriarch has too much power. Isabella's mother epitomizes the obedient, subjugated wife. She is a "model of conjugal nonentity" who "firmly believed that the husband ruled by divine right. . . . Such characters, if not interesting, are safe, provided they fall into good hands."[34] Because she is wholly dependent, Mrs. Linwood's marital subjugation creates an unstable and unreliable identity (she could easily be Frances Dunwoodie twenty years after her nuptials). She is a nonentity, and her mediated self-construction has made the act of standing up for anything, even her own children, nearly impossible. More ominously, her husband has developed tyrannical habits at least in part due to the inequality within his marriage—as he admits in conversation with Isabella. Because Mr. Linwood grew accustomed to wielding unquestioned power in the home, he is nearly incapable of dealing with divergent opinions in any aspect of his life, domestic or political. His dictatorial approach to inferiors causes him to alienate his only son and fly into fits of rage that demonstrate a dangerous lack of self-governance. Mr. Linwood blames his uncontrolled passions and self-indulgent lifestyle on his decision to marry someone he did not respect: "In a fit of pique I married your mother—mark the consequences. She has been the poor subservient, domestic drudge. . . . You can't dispute that I have been unreasonable, peevish, passionate, and so we have worn away life together."[35] A marriage that encouraged tyranny on one side and subjugation on the other led to dissipation and weakened self-will in both husband and wife. In *The Spy* Frances and Peyton Dunwoodie are an ideal pair because they fulfill the proper hierarchical positions in their relationship: Dunwoodie leads, Frances silently follows. In Sedgwick's book the Linwoods' marriage suggests that domestic relations built on a model of complete rule and absolute subservience render the patriarch and his subordinate unfit for rational participation in the public sphere.

Isabella Linwood's evolution into an American patriot requires her to rebel against her parents' values. Even her love interest stands in stark contrast to her father and the men celebrated by Cooper. While Isabella struggles for freedom from aristocratic mores, Eliot Lee joins the rebellion and progresses from farmer's son to military hero. Both characters develop over the course of the novel, emphasizing a capacity for growth and leadership in women and the middle classes. Cooper's hero, Peyton Dunwoodie, is an aristocratic slave-owning patriarch. Sedgwick's Eliot Lee is a middle-class farmer with egalitarian sensibilities. Dunwoodie does not evolve in the novel, nor does his position change. He begins the story as a brave major in love with Frances and ends the story as a brave major married to Frances. Cooper's representation of characters as largely static reinforces the message that intellect and leadership are stable qualities tied to a biologically determined identity. Sedgwick's hero Eliot Lee begins the novel as a college-educated member of the middling classes who is promoted during the war for bravery and his willingness to sacrifice for others. Eliot typifies a kind of civic virtue equally visible in Sedgwick's *Hope Leslie*, which as Maria Karafilis argues, "suggests that the dovetailing of individual and communal goods, the balancing of the tension between the individual and society, does not reflect an ordained harmonious, universal order but involves rebellion, adversarial action, and a profound human agency."[36] The source of Eliot Lee's leadership ability is not his aristocratic blood and upbringing; he is actuated instead by his strong will and community-sympathy. Like Isabella, Eliot ascribes to a distinctly feminized notion of civic virtue, and both characters are willing to rebel for the sake of these values. Isabella rejects society's expectations of an obedient Tory daughter while Eliot offers himself to the rebel cause.

Eliot's other relationships exemplify the androgynous ideal Phillip Gould associates with Sedgwick and with Lydia Maria Child's frontier romances, "at once feminizing republican manhood and coopting masculine political languages to invent female figures who carry domestic virtue into the public sphere."[37] This ideal is a direct rebuke to the dictatorial patriarchalism of Isabella's father. When Eliot departs for the war, the entire town shows up to give gifts and wish him well, actions born not just from admiration but also affection, speaking to him as members of an extended family. Kisel, a mentally handicapped young man who grew up with Eliot, recalls his childhood kindness: "When I boy, all boys laugh at me, knock me here, kick there—who took my part?—Misser Eliot, hey!"[38] Eliot's relationship with Kisel, who devotedly follows him into battle, predicts Eliot's domestic and political values. Though he attempts to guide Kisel and protects him when necessary, Eliot never denies Kisel autonomy. Despite Eliot's concerns, Kisel joins the army, which further tests Eliot's values. Herbert Linwood describes Eliot's shifting favor within the regiment in a letter to sister Isabella, recounting how Kisel's behavior threatened Eliot's ascension: "They had approached within gunshot of the works, when poor Kisel, who away from Eliot is like an unweaned child, and who had been all day wandering in search of him, suddenly emerged from the wood, and in a paroxysm of joy discharged his musket. Wayne sprang forward, and would have transfixed him with his bayonet, had not Eliot thrown himself before Kisel."[39] Herbert Linwood describes Kisel as a child and expresses surprise at Eliot's patience with him despite the possible damage to Eliot's military career. Eliot shows no compunction about caring for Kisel in a nurturing and supportive way, behavior considered more maternal than paternal in the early nineteenth century.

Eliot Lee represents the ideal republican leader because he pairs androgynous forms of domestic care with "the coolness and prudence of ripe age," a compliment offered to Eliot by the father of the nation, George Washington. In *The Linwoods*, emotion directed by rational self-governance enables individuals to act for the good of the community. Washington exemplifies these qualities: "It is well known that Washington's moderation and equanimity were the effects of the highest principle, not the gift of nature. He was constitutionally subject to gusts of passion, but he had acquired a power, almost divine (and doubtless from a divine source), by which he could direct the whirlwind and subdue the storm. A power that has seemed to the believing to verify that prophetic verse in Proverbs, which accords his natal day, and which truly graduates and expounds his virtues—'He that ruleth his own spirit is greater than he that taketh a city.'"[40] While promoting rational self-governance in this passage, Sedgwick's narrator notes that exercising such control is not a "gift of nature" determined at birth. It is a learned ability credited to God's presence and hard work. Even one of the greatest men in American history, born into the landed aristocracy, must contend with his natural passions. In *The Spy* aristocratic men demonstrate no such struggle while the lower classes consistently fail at self-mastery. This shift by Sedgwick strongly suggests that self-governance, a precursor of autonomous identity-formation and civic inclusion, is learned rather than biologically determined.

The most radical element of Sedgwick's republican vision lies in its focus on a woman's ability to develop and maintain the same traits that mark Eliot Lee for leadership. Like Eliot, Isabella's passion is matched by her ability to reason and act autonomously, both in the domestic and the political realms. Assessing separate-sphere rhetoric in historical literature, Linda K. Kerber links evolutions in republicanism with a challenge to patriarchal institutions. Christian discourse requiring women to police sexual licentiousness and other social sins was less than liberating, but it did imply that women were naturally "more self-controlled" than men.[41] Such rhetoric, which grew out of the rising valuation of private, middle-class virtues, challenged the associations between reason, masculinity, and self-mastery. Isabella demonstrates greater self-control and leadership potential than her father, brother, and early love interest, Jasper Meredith. All these men have been weakened by aristocratic upbringings; even Herbert, who has joined the revolutionary cause, often seems childish and self-interested. Sedgwick challenges the link between gender and self-mastery, representing irrational and uncontrolled passion as a symptom of an antidemocratic political ideology. Emily Van-Dette argues, based on brother-sister relationships in the novel, that Sedgwick promotes "the right to think and act independently only to those already enfranchised, and ask[s] them to use that power for the service and protection of their dependent, disenfranchised compatriots."[42] Dynamics in the Linwoods family contradict her claim. While it is true that Eliot protects his vulnerable younger sister, Isabella is the one who comes to her brother's aid and eventually reunites Herbert and their father after petulance on both their parts divides the family.

In large part *The Linwoods* is the story of Isabella's personal growth, which fortifies the lesson offered by Washington that self-governance is not a gift of nature but an ability developed by the individual, male or female. In the first scene Isabella is described as a natural leader with "an eye (albeit belong[ing] to one of the weaker sex) that looked as if she were born to empire." Marissa Carrere points out the hereditary element folded into these childhood scenes: "The novel works with competing investments in the child's capacity to configure the citizen-self's character as both born or natural and as unscripted or socially malleable."[43] The political ramifications of representing characters as socially malleable to any significant degree is clarified through consideration of *The Spy*. Representing female intellectual growth and celebrating social flux fundamentally challenges patriarchalism and, more generally, the notion that disenfranchised citizens are wholly incapable of moral autonomy. An important question posed by Sedgwick is how Isabella will use her natural ability to lead. Readers are introduced to two possible outcomes: self-interested manipulation of others to satisfy her needs, or sympathetic attendance to the needs of others. In the first scene, Isabella purposefully and cruelly frightens a superstitious male slave, Jape, with tales of slave hangings, solely for her own amusement.[44] It is also revealed in this chapter that Isabella urged relatively poor Bessie Lee's trip to the city purely to meet the innocent and sweet country girl her brother admired, treating Bessie as an object (a "rara avis") to be moved about at Isabella's will. The narrator also recounts Isabella's youthful effort to win freedom for a beloved family slave, Rose.[45] She makes a wager with her father on her ability to outperform classmates in the acquisition of French, a task she had been shirking: "The race was a hard one. . . . Isabella, hitherto a most desultory creature in her habits, and quitting her tasks at the slightest temptation, persevered like a Newton; and like all great spirits, she shaped destiny."[46] When motivated by a sympathetic understanding of Rose's desire for freedom, Isabella's self-discipline rises to match her natural abilities and she channels her powers into virtuous action. The inclusion of scenes that show Isabella's youthful unkindness reinforce the novel's sociopolitical message: people's character and beliefs are malleable. Isabella's evolution from a spirited but undisciplined girl into a woman who unites strong emotion with self-discipline and rational judgment makes her a model citizen.

Originally Isabella appears destined to marry Jasper Meredith, whose aristocratic biases lead him away from virtuous instincts and toward a self-interested, materialistic adulthood. In a pivotal scene Eliot, Isabella, Jasper, and the novel's female aristocrat Helen Ruthven (not coincidentally Jasper's eventual wife) attend a formal dinner at the loyalist Sir Henry's house. This dinner scene offers a dramatic revision of Cooper's encomium of etiquette in *The Spy*. Aristocratic loyalists at Sir Henry's dinner are weakly attached to finery and ostentation, while rebel soldiers demonstrate republican virtue by sacrificing comforts and risking their lives for the revolutionary cause. Isabella attends to fight for her brother's freedom, but what she observes that evening causes a political epiphany; it is at this dinner that Isabella becomes "American." Before entering the dining room, Isabella argues with Jasper about his seduction of Eliot's innocent young sister, Bessie Lee. Jasper does not seem capable of understanding Isabella's continuing loyalty to Bessie, whom he calls a "pretty little piece of rurality" who "relieved the inexpressible dullness of [his] position and pursuits."[47] After overhearing them, aristocrat Helen Ruthven engages in a defense of inconstancy, claiming that while the feeling matters, what you attach a feeling to is inconsequential (even if the "object" is a person). Shifting loyalties when it is convenient is perfectly reasonable. Helen's philosophy denigrates sustained attachments. In case the political implications of this speech are unclear, Helen later attempts to engineer George Washington's capture as he visits with her father, who is horrified by her duplicity. *The Spy* locates duplicity and inconstancy in the masses. Sedgwick repeatedly presents selfishness and disloyalty as aristocratic traits.

The dinner scene where Isabella, Eliot, Jasper, and Helen meet offers didactic commentary on republican virtue versus aristocratic self-interest. Sir Henry insults common Americans, calling merchants and men like Eliot "plebian," and belittles Isabella for interceding in political matters that a woman could not possibly understand. Isabella meanwhile comes to full recognition of her own loyalty to the American cause. She closely observes Eliot's interactions with their hosts. While they treat him as a subordinate, Eliot maintains a peaceful calm, comforted by "honest pride in being one among those who contracted for a glorious future, by the sacrifice of all animal and present indulgence. Dish after dish was removed and replaced, and the viands were discussed, and the generous wines poured out, as if to eat and to drink were the chief business and joy of life." When Eliot gives a rousing speech to the dinner party, Isabella is visibly moved and chimes in despite the dictates of etiquette. "Miss Linwood violated the strict rules that governed her contemporaries. She was not a lady of saws and precedents. But if she sometimes too impulsively threw open the door of her heart, there was nothing there exposed that could stain her cheek with a blush."[48] Isabella's transgression of propriety is glorified by Sedgwick rather than censured. Though self-government is essential, passion directed toward virtuous ends is not weakness. The aristocratic characters express more feeling for the food they are eating than for the suffering of their fellow men, showing the damage an aristocratic worship of luxury can do to the capacity for sympathy. Cooper praised attention to etiquette (including dress, dinner, and station) as keys to maintaining an ordered community, while Sedgwick portrays them as anything but community-building. Characters who overvalue etiquette in *The Linwoods* are too self-interested and materialistic to make the sacrifices that unify a community, nor can they be trusted to develop the rational self-governance essential to virtuous participation in the public sphere. Ultimately, Jasper Meredith and Helen Ruthven are consigned to a miserable marriage marked by competing self-interests. In the grand novelistic tradition of expelling undesirables from the nation, the novelist leaves them on a boat back to England.

Sedgwick closes her novel with the coupling of its two ideal republican citizens. The romantic revelation, that long-delayed moment when the hero and heroine confess their feelings, is peppered with unromantic language, fortifying the novel's vision of ideal domestic and national ties. More than anything, Eliot Lee stresses the rationality of his affection: "I am not now, nor was I ever, under the dominion of my imagination or my passions. I have been trained in the school of exertion, of self-denial, and self-subjection; and I would not, I could not love one who did not sway my reason."[49] This is no gothic drama, and Isabella Linwood will neither swoon nor faint. In a moment that reverses the relative positions of Cooper's hero and heroine, it is Eliot who throws himself at Isabella's feet. Marissa Carrere argues that in a novel that valorizes dissent, Eliot's and Sedgwick's like-minded political union "obscures the novel's more complicated investigations of disagreement."[50] Sedgwick does not challenge this convention of historical romance, within which a union marked by dissent would indeed have been radical. But few novels of this period offer such a scene. The heroine, whose personal and political growth centers the novel, agrees to marry Eliot because she comes to realize he is *her* equal. "She felt, for the first time, that there was that in Eliot Lee that could answer to the capacities of her own soul."[51] Isabella's response reasserts her autonomy even at this moment of union. Eliot's language echoes an earlier passage describing the revolution itself, which the narrator attributes to "the dignified resolve of thinking beings, not the angry impatience of overburdened animals."[52] In domestic and political terms, *The Linwoods* dismantles Cooper's vision of political subalterns as irrational and incapable of growth while simultaneously challenging a patriarchal relational model. Sociopolitical stability depends upon the efforts of individuals to develop their intellect and achieve self-governance rather than upon the ability of powerful leaders to control either their near-subordinates or the population en masse. This effort is no less necessary for George Washington than for Isabella Linwood.

Conclusion

James Fenimore Cooper and Catherine Maria Sedgwick mythologized the revolutionary war to promote stability and national pride. Their novels share a generic vocabulary, exploring the roles of emotion and reason, biological determinism, and class in the early republic while offering ideologically divergent visions of republicanism's future. Cooper's perspective on democracy and republicanism is a matter of scholarly debate, but his conservatism is apparent. Corey Robin's description of the animus that drives conservatives could grace the back of Cooper's books as a promotional blurb: "Conservativism is the theoretical voice of this animus against the agency of the subordinate classes. It provides the most consistent and profound argument as to why the lower orders should not be allowed to exercise their independent will, why they should not be allowed to govern themselves or the polity. Submission is their first duty, agency, the prerogative of the elite."[53] Cooper's work calls not just for maintaining the status quo but also for a return to classical republicanism and a silencing of those who want a more democratic nation. For Cooper, the ideal domestic/political organization requires monolithic leadership: wives, workers, and slaves follow the white patriarch's lead and support his rational endeavors. Central to this conception is Cooper's fearful representation of mobile identities. Fluidity, the possibility of individual growth for subaltern populations, represents a threat to what made America great. The nostalgia of this rhetoric stands out as particularly anxious for a twenty-first-century reader. When *The Spy* was published, the United States had been an independent nation for only forty years. Conservativism is fundamentally reactionary, and its fervency comes from the fear that significant change looms on the horizon—change that could shift sociopolitical power in meaningful ways. Cooper's anxiety-riddled commentaries on the masses, the press, and the disappearing respect for social station illustrate a broader feeling that, like it or not, political subalterns were gaining a voice in the nation.

Cooper warns his fellow citizens. "There is now no enemy to fear, but the one that resides within. By accustoming ourselves to regard even the people as erring beings, and by using the restraints that wisdom has adduced from experience, there is much reason to hope that the same Providence which has so well aided us in our infancy, may continue to smile on our manhood."[54] In *The Linwoods* the greatest enemy to stability lies not within the broad polity but within each individual whose duty is to develop a capacity for self-governance. Sedgwick's emphasis on rational deliberation aligns with classical notions of republican virtue, but she contests another central premise: that reason and moral autonomy are the exclusive province of patriarchs. She offers this challenge to conservative views while representing aristocratic mores as the greatest threat to reason and virtue, thus extending to political subalterns the possibility of civic subjectivity and discursive participation. She promotes, as did eighteenth-century female abolitionists in Great Britain, the productive possibilities of a more diverse public sphere. In a critique of liberal theories, Habermas takes issue with the failure to understand "that those to whom the law is addressed can acquire autonomy (in the Kantian sense) only to the extent that they can understand themselves as the authors of the laws to which they are subject."[55] For disenfranchised citizens, participation in the political public sphere offers a form of public autonomy denied them by discriminatory laws. Sedgwick and Cooper demonstrate an evocative awareness of the power that can be wrested out of the modern discursive public sphere, as well as the stakes involved in deciding who can and cannot be a virtuous citizen and rightful participant.

"Possessed with an Idea"

American Abolitionism and Counterpublic Protest

In eighteen-century England Anna Laetitia Barbauld and other counterpublic activists challenged the idea that virtuous citizenship entails service or sacrifice to the state. In "True Heroism," Barbauld depicts military leaders as false idols and attributes the highest order of courage and virtue to Tom, a young man who sacrifices his body and health to support his suffering mother, favoring private over public heroism. In "Civic Sermons to the People," she concurrently urged members of the general population to educate themselves and to hold the government accountable when it fails to act ethically. The American abolition movement pushed the discourse of virtuous citizenship a step further, adopting classical understanding of republican virtue as self-sacrifice to valorize protest against state-sanctioned injustices. Writers like Harriet Martineau and Harriet Beecher Stowe represent moral fortitude as an outgrowth of privately constituted, publicly defended principles. In multiple books and essays, Martineau describes abolitionists as those willing to martyr themselves to the fight for freedom, while Stowe dramatizes the steadfast virtue of Christian women, slaves, and religious separatists in the face of a coldly pragmatic and threatening power structure. They each represent self-sacrifice as a central component of civic virtue. Nobility and honor, however, are not found through defense of the nation but in acts of bravery inspired by commitment to ideals, both personal and political.

Abolitionists were not the only antebellum authors whose work promoted commitment to personal morals in public life as essential to virtuous republicanism in early America. In *The American Scholar* Ralph Waldo Emerson describes the estimable "Man Thinking" as one who develops independent values and willingly speaks out about those ideals regardless of external pressure.[1] Friend and fellow transcendentalist Henry David Thoreau in "Resistance to Civil Government" represents a refusal to pay taxes and a willingness to be jailed as morally courageous ways to protest political injustices. Though these works illustrate widespread discourse on moral fortitude and civic virtue in early American literature, they are not the focus of my analysis because the rhetoric within elides the necessity of a public community to make individual moral courage politically efficacious. Emerson's scholar, a role Thoreau assumes, will help guide men, but such virtue belongs to exceptional individuals. Thoreau describes his fellow citizens as generally incapable of standing up for what is morally right if it means sacrificing comfort. In *Walden* Thoreau pursues a moral life through social separatism, demonstrating his ability to live independently on property owned by Emerson. This vision of autonomy and virtue ignores one of the most important components of work that promotes true democratization: the public sphere's capacity to expand participation through community-building.

Neither Emerson nor Thoreau faced any legal limitation to their rights as citizens, placing them squarely inside the nation's civic body. Those marginalized by race, gender, or economic status need authorizing communities to attain political efficacy. As Seyla Benhabib argues, "Political actors need bounded communities—whether they be cities, religions, states, or transnational institutions—within which they can establish mechanisms of representation, accountability, participation, and deliberation."[2] For early nineteenth-century US political subalterns, the state did not provide such a space. Slaves had no legal civil existence; women, children, and other dependents were submembers through their connection to autonomous paternal figures.[3] This chapter focuses on antislavery literature because in its depiction of the abolitionist community as exemplars of moral fortitude and courage, it deals with more than just the individual capacity to be ethical citizens. It promotes counterpublic community-formation, a space wherein marginalized citizens can develop civic identities and public-sphere authority. Although abolitionists like William Lloyd Garrison met the Aristotelian requirements of a free citizen, neither owning property nor living a "life free from necessity" were required for membership in abolitionist circles.

The ideological split between Thoreau and abolitionist authors such as Harriet Martineau and Harriet Beecher Stowe echoes the basic distinction between a liberal-versus-republican conception of the individual's relationship to the nation. Liberalism emphasizes individual rights and sees the government's role as protector of those rights. Republicanism adds a component of community membership and responsibility on the part of citizens.[4] Habermas argues that liberal philosophers often fail to acknowledge socialization's central role in the production or experience of real autonomy. In order to feel fully a part of the law, one must have some part in its creation. "Persons, including legal persons, become individualized only through a process of socialization. A correctly understood theory of rights requires a politics of recognition that protects the integrity of the individual in the life-contexts in which his or her identity is formed." Habermas credits "social movements and political struggles" with creating this possibility.[5] I argue that eighteenth- and nineteenth-century counterpublics provided an essential space for disenfranchised citizens to build such identities. They created ideologically bound communities wherein political subalterns could raise their voices, providing the social recognition necessary for civic autonomy.

Though Benhabib focuses on sociopolitical changes after 1948, what she writes about the experience of democracy and the shape of the demos applies in illuminating ways to the nineteenth century. Counterpublic movements were increasingly transnational, and in the case of abolitionism, united more fully by a cosmopolitan set of values than by shared religious, racial, or gender identities. Benhabib points out the mutability of the demos and the role played by civic life in defining membership within a democracy. "Democratic rule, unlike imperial dominion, is exercised in the name of some specific constituency and binds that constituency alone. Therefore, at the same time that the sovereign defines itself territorially, it also defines itself in civic terms. Those who are full members of the sovereign body are distinguished from those who 'fall under its protection,' but who do not enjoy 'full membership rights.'"[6] In the nineteenth century, women, children, and nonpropertied freemen fell under the protection of paternalistic figures. Slaves were treated as entirely outside of the demos. When activists form counterpublic communities, their work concurrently alters the demos by changing the boundaries of civic belonging. Every time someone not considered a full member of the sovereign body engages in protest and speaks out about change, they challenge limitations on civic inclusion.

Harriet Martineau's work exemplifies the transnational and ideologically driven elements of nineteenth-century counterpublics. Though British, she was deeply involved in American abolitionism, and unlike other well-known female participants in the abolition movement, her rhetoric was less about a shared Christian identity than about her commitment to increased freedom for all members of society. She embodies the capacity of political counterpublics to provide an affiliation apart from those already offered by civil society.[7] Martineau promotes the view that civic virtue lies not in citizens' defense of the nation against external threats but in their willingness to sacrifice themselves and court danger based on commitment to social ideals, against which citizens should measure the official sphere's commercial and political practices.[8] Martineau portrays engagement in this battle as the pinnacle of civic virtue. Harriet Beecher Stowe's fiction provides a sentimental illustration of this belief. Steadfast virtue is embodied by characters without official-sphere roles, people who exist almost entirely outside the demos or as dependents within it. Stowe's virtuous characters, like Martineau's real-life abolitionists, are compelled to action by commitment to principles—freedom, sympathy, and religious faith—rather than to the nation itself. This is the apotheosis of the ongoing transformation of civic virtue, which promoted the need for private virtue in public sphere life: Citizens who are prepared to court danger within the nation for the sake of social justice are celebrated as republican martyrs.

Sarah Josepha Hale's *Northwood*, first published in 1826 as an expressly antislavery work, was reissued in 1852 with a new agenda: a rebuke to abolitionists, whom she sees as a threat to national unity. It is also a response to those, like Martineau, who define civic virtue as a commitment to immutable values rather than loyalty to the state. For Hale, the virtuous citizen above all other considerations devotes herself to the unity and stability of the United States, a country destined to Christianize the world. Despite its explicit call to traditional views of republican virtue, I argue *Northwood* presents an ideology-based vision of membership in the demos. Like abolitionists, Hale promotes the growth of a transnational community committed to altering the nation, calling for the expulsion of African Americans from the United States in order to make room for Anglo-Saxons fleeing the moral turpitude of decadent cultures. Sarah Josepha Hale is still regularly celebrated as a paragon of nineteenth-century patriotism—she fought for decades to see Thanksgiving become a national holiday and finally succeeded in 1863. *Northwood* demonstrates that Hale's primary commitment was to an ideological vision of the nation's future, one no less transformative than the version abolitionists were fighting to create.

FREEDOM AND DEMOCRACY: HARRIET MARTINEAU'S ANGLO-ATLANTIC AFFILIATIONS

Many English writers participated in the abolitionist cause and maintained transatlantic relationships with American activists during the antebellum era, but it would be difficult to find a writer more impassioned or prolific than Harriet Martineau. In 1834, after gaining sudden fame as the author of *Illustrations of Political Economy*, a series of stories illustrating economic theories for the general public, Martineau departed for a two-year tour of America. Martineau had access to past presidents, including James Madison and Thomas Jefferson; well-known writers such as Catharine Maria Sedgwick and Henry Wadsworth Longfellow; and key figures in the abolition movement, including Lydia Maria Child and Maria Weston Chapman, the latter of whom became a lifelong friend and correspondent. From these experiences, Martineau wrote *Society in America*, in which she analyzes American politics, the economy, slavery, the status of women, and other sociopolitical issues. The book is often touted as one of the first sociological studies. In 1838 Martineau published *Retrospect of Western Travel*, a more traditional travel book, and that same year added a sociological theory tract, *How to Observe Morals and Manners*. She also wrote "The Martyr Age of the United States," a novella-length article on American abolitionism. Her discursive participation in transatlantic public sphere debates regarding republicanism, slavery, and women's rights would continue unabated through the Civil War.[9]

Society in America, which contains the germs of Martineau's philosophy of civic virtue, demonstrates her passionate commitment to freedom, equality, and democratic republicanism. Martineau's vision of civic virtue emerges most clearly in "The Martyr Age," her paean to abolitionists. But her description of an ethical methodology for sociopolitical study in *Society in America* laid the groundwork. Martineau differentiates herself from British travel writers who had maligned the United States based on British cultural norms. Instead of measuring US politics and society against other nations, Martineau compares "the existing state of society in America with the principles on which it is professedly founded."[10] Martineau claims that this methodology guarantees objectivity because its source is the stated resolutions of the US Constitution and the Declaration of Independence. The standard against which the US should be measured is the *idea* of democratic republicanism as described in its founding documents. Critiques of the nation, when they arise, are derived from internal inconsistencies rather than comparison with other nations. This methodology, in addition to supporting Martineau's professed objectivity, parallels her depiction of virtuous citizenship. Virtuous citizens and nations demonstrate moral autonomy through their performance of individually or privately held values.

Martineau largely follows this methodology in *Society in America*, but her political biases emerge in transnational comparisons that demonstrate her commitment to democracy and warn against potential damage when inequality goes unchecked. Throughout the book her criticism of America centers on the ways in which the nation fails to challenge the aristocratic legacies of England. In her indictments of slavery and the inequality of women, Martineau's most vitriolic critiques are frequently leveled against Europe. Discussing the degradation of marriage in America versus that in England, Martineau slips into a virulent indictment of European society: "Nothing like a comparison between one country and another in different circumstances can be instituted: nor would any one desire to enter upon such a comparison. The bottomless vice, the all-pervading corruption of European society cannot, by possibility, be yet paralleled in America."[11] A new, avowedly democratic republic represents an opportunity to build a nation that might base its political and social systems on virtuous first principles. Ultimately, Martineau's critiques of Europe and the United States suggest that her civic affiliation is to neither nation but rather to the principles of liberty and democracy, a devotion that aligned her with American abolitionists.[12]

R. K. Webb characterizes Harriet Martineau's view of American society as "limited, naive, even at times embarrassing" and disapprovingly compares her idealistic attitude toward the Constitution and the Declaration of Independence to the outlook of real American citizens. "Where the Americans took the Declaration as a formula and an excuse for raucous piety on the Fourth of July, Harriet Martineau took it literally and, as she had done with political economy, reduced it to absurdity." Martineau is like those thoughtlessly flag-waving Americans, with an equally passionate and almost equally shallow comprehension of complex political matters. But Webb's analysis misses an essential point: Martineau's belief in the transformative capacity of idealism. Martineau's respect for what the Declaration of Independence and Constitution represent and make possible, and her faith in the progress that would result from an educated general public engaged in democratic governance, are anything but simple. Martineau's optimism was the practical manifestation of a thoughtful and complex political philosophy. Within this newly emerging form of civic life, one that emphasized a shared commitment to ideals and existed most powerfully in counterpublics, maintaining some idealism was necessary. Fighting injustice from outside the mainstream civic body and sustaining like-minded but diverse public sphere communities without such shared beliefs and commitments would be formidable if not impossible.[13]

For Martineau faith in democracy and the demos itself was essential to sociopolitical progress. It was "the imaginative political character of the Americans" that allowed the possibility for the righting of wrongs and the resolution of continuing social inequalities. Martineau describes this romantic political character:

> I regard the American people as a great embryo poet: now moody, now wild, but bringing out results of absolute good sense . . . exulting that he has caught the true aspect of things past, and at the depth of futurity which lies before him, wherein to create something so magnificent as the world has scarcely begun to dream of. There is the strongest hope of a nation that is capable of being possessed with an idea; and this kind of possession has been the peculiarity of the Americans from their first day of national existence till now. The American people have not only much to learn, and a painful discipline to endure, but some disgraceful faults to repent of and amend. They must give a perpetual and earnest heed to one point; to cherish their high democratic hope, their faith in man. The older they grow, the more must they 'reverence the dreams of their youth.' They must eschew the folly and profaneness so prevalent in the old world, of exalting man, abstractedly and individually, as a piece of God's creation, and despising men in the mass.[14]

The cynicism of denigrating the masses is what New World republicanism must shed in order to progress toward a society that values equality and justice. If the American people can maintain this poetic political soul, then the aberrations in their system (most significantly slavery and lack of suffrage for women) will be resolved by those who possess a democratic genius that can only thrive in a nation where idealism trumps pragmatism, a nation possessed with an idea.

This passage reveals the symbiotic relationship between Harriet Martineau's radical political philosophy and the United States. In the 1830s Martineau traveled to a country whose own authors were engaged in the work of literary nationalism. Even for writers such as James Fenimore Cooper who reflect distrust of the masses, there is faith in and hope for the nation's future, and a belief that individual citizens participating in public discourse have some power in dictating its shape. In *The Linwoods*, which was published while Martineau was in the United

States, Sedgwick's faith in the masses and investment in democratization is evident. For Martineau, the stagnant and historically weighted Old World was more difficult ground for this type of generative, imaginative political spirit. What Webb described as naïveté was actually Martineau's effort to practice what she preached.[15] She would hold the United States accountable for the goals proposed in its founding documents and encourage the citizens' political imagination, their belief in the ideal not yet realized. Martineau located the civic power of a republican populace in hope, faith, dreams, and imagination rather than in martial power, property, and stability. Martineau's central philosophy reflects the necessary components of counterpublic formation: commitment to a shared ideal and purpose as well as the ability and willingness to imagine oneself as connected to an amorphous and transnational group of like-minded individuals.

In "The Martyr Age of the United States" Martineau increased abolitionists' moral capital by portraying them as exemplars of republican virtue willing to sacrifice even their lives for the cause. Martineau's choice of the term *martyr* represents the apex of self-sacrifice, a willingness to face death in defense of one's faith. Her description of William Lloyd Garrison typifies this reverence. Garrison is "one of God's nobility—the head of the moral aristocracy whose prerogatives we are contemplating . . . his meekness, his sympathies, his self-forgetfulness, he appears 'covered all over with the stars and orders' of the spiritual realm whence he derives his dignities and powers." Martineau's beatification of Garrison reflects her admiring words in *Society in America* for the revolutionary spirit that won America its independence. She describes those fighting against slavery in terms associated with ideal republican citizenship and revolutionary valor. Abolitionists such as Maria Weston Chapman and the Grimke sisters gave up worldly advantages and accepted social exclusion for the sake of their cause. William Lloyd Garrison barely escapes being tarred by the gentlemen of Boston.[16]

Elizabeth Spelman calls into question the end result of martyrological abolitionist discourse and challenges the common description of slavery as the great American tragedy. She points out that such rhetoric represents slavery as a singular flaw, thereby discouraging an honest assessment of the racism and inequality built into American democracy. Martineau's work seemingly exemplifies this trope in abolitionist rhetoric. Martineau often celebrates the revolutionary generation's commitment to freedom and liberty despite knowing that many signers of the Declaration of Independence not only supported slavery but also owned slaves themselves. Taken as a whole, Martineau's writing reflects Spelman's contention that abolitionists represented slavery as a "flaw in the founding vision of America but that it is otherwise noble and powerful." Yet early in "The Martyr Age," Martineau acknowledges that "slavery is as thoroughly interwoven with American institutions—ramifies as extensively through American society, as the aristocratic spirit pervades Great Britain."[17] In all her work, Martineau straddles the line between critical assessments of injustice and the idealism she believed necessary to move the needle of liberty. Idealization in "The Martyr Age" serves a particular political purpose. The recitation of abolitionist sacrifices, celebration of their bravery, and comparison to American revolutionary heroes represent Martineau's effort to attract new adherents to a cause that could lead to arrest or worse. Redefining republican virtue to honor protest creates moral capital for a movement consistently represented as viciously set on social destruction.

Martineau's work promotes devotion to a political cause as a central means for virtuous civic community building. Abolitionists "act as if they were of one heart and of one soul. Such union could be secured by no principle of worldly interest. . . . A well-grounded faith, directed towards a noble object, is the only principle which can account" for this commitment. Abolitionists are united by shared affective and spiritual principles, and they derive moral autonomy from the power of these beliefs. Martineau compares American abolitionists to citizens in Great Britain who fight against the aristocratic institutions that contaminate every aspect of society, demonstrating once again that she saw herself as part of a transnational community bound by shared fundamental ideals. Martineau's writing relies upon the trope of Christian sacrifice but ultimately reads as a secular celebration of republican virtue. Discussing Martineau's description of John Brown, Ted Hovet captures her approach to martyrdom. "Even if she depicts Brown as a Christ figure, it is not so much an eschatological claim about religious matters but a suggestion that in Brown's death rests the opportunity for America to redeem itself and fulfill its worldly principles."[18] Throughout the book Martineau affiliates herself with Old- and New-World citizens who are dedicated to expanding democracy. The citizens who make up this virtuous counterpublic represent a broad swath of the population: enfranchised and disenfranchised, black and white, men and women. Martineau's description of abolition communities is an effort to promote and expand a transnational, ideologically driven political counterpublic.

There is political efficacy to be gained in female abolitionists' efforts to wrest the terms of civic virtue from the ruling class, a class Martineau represents as avaricious, a trait that damages their moral autonomy. She lingers on the status of those who censure and threaten female abolitionists and who attack Garrison, contrasting the virtuous marginalized civic community with those in power fighting to maintain the status quo. The attack on Garrison happened the same evening a mob gathered to prevent the Boston Female Anti-Slavery Society from meeting, betraying their anxiety about the group's possible growth and impact.[19] Martineau rode through the streets of Boston in a carriage that night, a witness to the attack. She informs her readers that this mob consisted of the "gentlemen" of the city: "The fear for the purses of the merchants and ship-owners of the North was becoming exasperated into panic. . . . The lawyers and clergy, 'gentlemen of property and standing' of every sort, and the press, gave their sympathy to the merchants, and the result was presently visible in the reflection of flames upon the midnight sky. The American reign of terror now began."[20] Martineau compares the wealthy citizens of Boston to the ungovernable mobs of the French Revolution, reversing rhetoric that locates instability and violence in the protesting masses. These antiabolitionist, property-owning pillars of the nation burn down houses, churches, and schools, the sacred domestic and public spaces of a democratic republic. In *Society in America* Martineau refers to this behavior and its effects as "the tyranny of the monied mob."[21] The actions of the leading classes (attributed explicitly to their greed) are grim, but Martineau holds out hope for the republic itself. She describes a positive cycle in towns throughout the north.

Abolitionism increases, the monied mobs form out of fear, violence ensues and must be countered. This cycle inspires antislavery sentiment in the nation's youth. Having learned from the leaders ahead of them, the next generation votes an abolitionist candidate into office. In the end, although greed holds sway over those in power, moral understanding and the love of freedom inform the masses. In a republican nation where no one is guaranteed the right of political leadership through inherited power, that understanding and love will keep the country moving in the direction of virtue. Martineau's narrative of progress establishes a dialectic between the center and the margins, identifying official-sphere leaders as corrupt and placing civic virtue and responsibility squarely in the hands of political subalterns uncorrupted by inherited power and committed to the ideals of freedom, liberty, and equality.

Uncle Tom's Cabin: Civic Virtue versus Sociopolitical Pragmatism

Leslie Fiedler has called *Uncle Tom's Cabin* "the greatest of all novels of sentimental protest." While Fiedler's analysis is engagingly hyperbolic at times, including her claim that the "chief pleasure" of Stowe's novel is "rooted not in the moral indignation of the reformer but in the more devious titillations of the sadist," her celebration of the novel's position in protest literature and discussion of martyrology remain pertinent. An upsurge in analysis of Stowe's novel began soon after Fiedler folded it into her broad study, with feminist scholars leading the charge. Since then *Uncle Tom's Cabin* has been a linchpin for analysis of the racial and gender politics in abolitionist discourse. In "Heroines in Uncle Tom's Cabin," Elizabeth Ammons links Stowe's matriarchal ethic to Christian self-sacrifice. The Christ-like lives of Tom and Eva "offer an unmasculine ideal for all human behavior."[22] Other critics, including Gillian Brown, Jane Tompkins, Jean Yellin Fagan, and Lori Ginzberg, have argued that the revisionist and revolutionary politics of Stowe's sentimental novel lie primarily in the challenge it offers to patriarchal values, including its celebration of benevolence, self-sacrifice, and "salvation through motherly love."[23] These critics convincingly established not just the protofeminist element of Stowe's work but also the extent to which it challenged the rhetoric of separate spheres, exposing the inextricability of domestic and political life. For those interested in better understanding widely consumed political fiction during the antebellum era, no text is more significant than *Uncle Tom's Cabin*. Its sales numbers in the nineteenth century would make it a best seller even today. Stowe's critique of patriarchal institutions, her challenge to separate spheres, and her celebration of virtue in the political margins promote counterpublic activism.

Uncle Tom's Cabin carries echoes of Harriet Martineau's work, reflecting a shared conviction that civic virtue and sociopolitical progress grow out of passionate commitment to ideals.[24] The characters who demonstrate social sympathy and moral fortitude (with few exceptions) are women, slaves, children, or Quakers.[25] Corruption, alternatively, adheres to commercially and politically powerful white males. Whether virtuous or vicious in their domestic lives, these men leave questions of morality at the door when engaging in business or politics. Stowe offers an important perspective on the power of the public sphere and, more specifically, the democratic role played by counterpublics. Arendt and Habermas argue that the rise of personal self-interest through reputation-management in democratic republics has degraded the public sphere's political role. Stowe suggests that this problem exists most significantly in the dominant public sphere, the realm inhabited by those who already have governing power. She critiques those in business and politics who behave unethically and then rationalize their actions by claiming that in the world, unlike in the home, such compromise is necessary. Members of the abolitionist counterpublic, constituted almost entirely by political subalterns, withstand the temptation to sacrifice virtue to self-interest. By portraying disenfranchised citizens this way, Stowe promotes a positive view of counterpublics' role in national progress, showing that networks of like-minded, politically marginalized people can and should use their moral strength to change the nation's political landscape.

The opening scene introduces readers to Mr. Shelby, Tom's owner, and Haley, the slave trader who has accepted Tom as partial payment on a debt. Their interactions and shared perspective of business show the pervasive moral corruption that attends slavery. Mr. Shelby represents a Kentucky gentleman. His speech and appearance are cultivated, and he treats his slaves humanely. He is the husband of a compassionate, educated Christian woman and father to a sweet-natured, spirited young man. Kenneth Hada argues Mr. Shelby's "good intentions are thwarted by economics evidently beyond his control," and David S. Reynolds similarly describes him as a goodhearted victim of capitalism. The opening scene alone begs for a harsher assessment of Shelby's readiness to abandon Christian virtue, as does the fact that Shelby's financial need arose because he "speculated largely and quite loosely."[26] Instead of exculpating him, Mr. Shelby's kind nature and model domesticity make his and Haley's similar attitudes toward business all the more potent a critique of an economic system that relies on literal dehumanization, linking it to broader moral degradation in politics and business. During negotiations, Mr. Shelby questions Haley's conscience. Haley's response is pragmatic: "I've got just as much conscience as any man in business can afford to keep,—just a little, you know, to swear by." He measures the necessity for a conscience based on its exchange value. In the slave trade, Haley's words insinuate, this value is extremely limited. Though Mr. Shelby condescendingly criticizes Haley, his own defense for trading Tom echoes Haley's rationale. Asked by Mrs. Shelby to justify the sale of Tom and Eliza's young son Harry, Mr. Shelby insists he is only doing what any man in his situation would do. When his wife reminds Shelby that he earlier critiqued their minister's exculpatory proslavery sermon, he explains, "We men of the world must wink pretty hard at various things, and get used to a deal that isn't the exact thing. But we don't quite fancy, when women and ministers come out broad and square, and go beyond us in matters of either modesty or morals, that's a fact. But now, my dear, I trust you see the necessity of the thing, and you see that I have done the very best that circumstances would allow."[27] While ministers and women should uphold virtue, businessmen in the United States cannot be held to such standards. Participating successfully in the commercial sphere is only possible with a pragmatic understanding that vice sometimes must be winked at. Stowe's antislavery novel condemns this view and suggests that without an infusion of virtue from women, dissenters, and slaves themselves, the economic and political spheres will remain corrupt.

Mr. Shelby's attitude toward private virtue in public life differs very little from Haley's partial conscience. Haley, who makes decisions based solely on economic imperatives, is the end result of a market-driven ethos. As Mr. Shelby explains to his wife, Haley is "not a cruel man, exactly, but a man of leather,—a man alive to nothing but trade and profit,—cool, and unhesitating, and unrelenting, as death and the grave. He'd sell his own mother at a good per centage—not wishing the old woman any harm, either." There is no sacred domestic in Haley's worldview: his commitment to financial gain leaves no room for competing affiliations. On a ship headed to the slave market, Lucy, one of Haley's acquisitions, jumps overboard after discovering that Haley has sold her baby. Her fellow slave Tom is deeply saddened by what he observes, but Lucy's death elicits only self-pity in Haley. "The trader . . . sat discontentedly down, with his little account-book, and put down the missing body and soul under the head of *losses*!"[28] One of Stowe's direct addresses follows this scene. The narrator reminds readers that the "enlightened, cultivated, intelligent man" who owns slaves or continues to support the system has created this inhumane band of traders whose population is growing. Shelby tells his wife he must sell Tom and Harry to save the farm, but Stowe's narrator notes that gambling debts forced this sale, which results in Tom's murder at the hands of the brutal slave owner Simon Legree. Despite his kindness to slaves, the influence of a pious wife, and his status as a gentleman, Mr. Shelby willingly winks at immoral deeds rather than applying private virtue to public activities, which would disrupt his economic goals. Mr. Shelby is only a victim of the economic system because he is unwilling to even nominally sacrifice his personal comfort for the greater good, a fact that implies the absence of both moral autonomy and civic virtue.

Stowe's indictment of official-sphere pragmatism extends to politics and to the North through a brief but pointed scene inside the home of an Ohio senator. Senator Bird demonstrates more domestic devotion to Christian values than Mr. Shelby and is not a slave owner himself. His willingness to detach political actions from personal morals potently signals a widespread ethical failure of American businessmen and politicians as well as a failure of the slavery-tainted public sphere to encourage virtuous behavior. The example of Senator Bird also communicates a dilemma developing in the US due to amoral politics. When those in power pass or support laws that punish sympathy and benevolence, citizens must either turn away from virtue entirely, like Tom's malevolent master Simon Legree, wink at hypocrisies and run from guilt, like Mr. Shelby, or live outside the law. Readers meet Senator Bird arriving home after helping create and pass a law that echoes the Fugitive Slave Act. Mrs. Bird, who resembles Mrs. Shelby in character (she is a pious, loving, and rational presence in the marriage and home) immediately criticizes her husband for failing to promote their domestic values in his public role. Essentially, Mrs. Bird argues, this new law makes it illegal to practice the Christian principles of benevolence and sympathy. Mr. Bird does not disagree with his wife, but his response recalls Mr. Shelby: "Your feelings are all quite right, dear, and interesting, and I love you for them; but, then, dear, we mustn't suffer our feelings to run away with our judgment; you must consider it's not a matter of private feelings,—there are great public interests involved."[29] Mr. Shelby and the kindhearted Senator Bird both assert that applying private values to public activities is impractical. Strict attendance to Christian virtues disrupts the more important goals of compromise and stability. Government and business in the United States are fueled by pragmatism, not ideals. In *Uncle Tom's Cabin* Stowe continues the work of eighteenth-century British abolitionists by showing how damaging this detachment can be to the spirit of the nation. She also echoes Harriet Martineau's call for idealism over cynicism. It is time, Stowe argues, for our feelings to play a more active role in public life and political judgment. By passing laws to appease slaveholders, America's political leaders participate in the degradation of both political and private life. Mr. Bird offers Eliza a bed, his deceased son's clothes, and money, then transports her to a safe house. This moment of legal transgression by a US senator suggests that in the long term, national virtue requires the application of private virtue to public life, and in the short term, political dissent is more virtuous than obedience to the state.

For Mr. Bird and Mr. Shelby, questions of virtue and sympathy have no place in the public sphere though they are lauded in the domestic space. Stowe's novel shows this position is corrosive and unsustainable. The laws of government and the conduct of businessmen infiltrate these homes, deconstructing their attempts to excuse public-sphere immorality through the reification of private-sphere virtue. Tom and the other slaves on Mr. Shelby's farm refer to themselves as Shelby's "people." Mrs. Shelby, who consistently refers to them as family, teaches them to respect Christian principles, practice honesty, and value family ties. When Tom's family is torn apart and Harry is sold because of Mr. Shelby's business practices, the domestic virtues inculcated by Mrs. Shelby are degraded, a fact she protests: "I have taught them the duties of the family, of parent and child, and husband and wife; and how can I bear to have this open acknowledgement that we care for no tie, no duty, no relation, however sacred, compared with money?" Kenneth Hada is correct when he argues that "Stowe primarily appropriates virtue with the female in the novel and the evils of the market with men."[30] She exposes the market's multifaceted infiltration of home life in a nation that maintains domestic slavery. Utilitarian and market considerations decide who remains in Shelby's so-called family and who is traded away. Mrs. Shelby's idealism is no match for political reality, which lives in her home as much as the marketplace. Representing public and private life as intertwined in this way furthers the message that private virtue must have a place in business and politics. Otherwise readers should be prepared to see corruption infiltrate their homes.

Some characters refuse to conform to the market ethic, which judges the success or efficacy of a choice based on economic considerations. Most of them are political subalterns, citizens with limited rights, or slaves, who have no authorized civic identity. Mrs. Shelby in particular represents virtuous Christian matriarchal leadership. When she attempts to find a way to bring Tom home, Mr. Shelby silences his wife: first, by stating that women never understand business, second, by speaking over her. Mrs. Shelby stops speaking when she realizes her husband will not listen, and Stowe's narrator highlights the injustice of this dismissal: "The fact was, that though her husband had stated she was a woman, she had a clear, energetic, practical mind, and a force of character every way superior to that of her husband; so that it would not have been so very absurd a supposition, to have allowed her capable of managing, as Mr. Shelby supposed."[31] Mrs. Shelby and Mrs. Bird combine a commitment to practical management with Christian virtues. Mrs. Shelby also demonstrates fortitude and a willingness to make personal sacrifices for the communal good, qualities associated with America's revolutionary war heroes and central to early American visions of the ideal republican. Mr. Shelby leaves town the weekend Tom is taken south to avoid the guilt he could not entirely escape. Mrs. Shelby stays home to help comfort Tom's wife, Chloe, and say goodbye to Tom, a sympathetic act that eases the slave's pain and anger. Mrs. Shelby also offers to take on work so they can afford to bring Tom home. In Stowe's book Christian women, slaves, and religious dissenters speak up about injustice. They act according to their professed values to create a more virtuous nation.

Stowe's feminine ethical domestic manager and corrupt masculine sociopolitical leader suggest that the contemporary state of public morals negatively affects those in power and that progress toward a moral society requires the application of private virtue to public life.[32] When Mr. Shelby dies his estate passes into his wife's hands. "Mrs. Shelby, with characteristic energy, applied herself to the work of straightening the entangled web of affairs; and she and George were for some time occupied with collecting and examining accounts, selling property and settling debts; for Mrs. Shelby was determined that everything should be brought into tangible and recognizable shape."[33] In addition to ably handling the financial problems left behind by her husband, Mrs. Shelby initiates a search for Tom. After his death she and son George free all the slaves, offering them jobs as paid laborers on the farm. From early childhood, George showed an affinity for his mother's principles and sympathy for Tom and the other slaves. He and his mother work together to remove the corruption of slavery from their household. In so doing, they create a virtuous home.

George Shelby as the hero of this novel, however, offers an incomplete and unsatisfying conclusion. He exists offstage for most of the novel, nor is he the inheritor of power who most exemplifies heroic action in *Uncle Tom's Cabin*. That role belongs to the women who challenge patriarchal political values and the slaves who maintain a passionate commitment to their beliefs despite vicious treatment and constant threat of death. It is Tom's passing that inspires George Shelby to abandon the chattel-slave system he inherited. As Jane Tompkins attests, death is powerful in the novel because it offers others redemption. While the empowerment offered by Tom's passivity and martyrdom has been called into question with good reason, Mark Miller's analysis of abolitionist martyrology places Tom in the context of contemporary rhetoric. Stowe's work granted Tom a level of agency and purpose uncommon in the work of her male activist counterparts. He demonstrates a "self-willed determination to suffer," resisting Simon Legree's attempts to debase him and offering a spiritual, family-oriented counter to the stereotype of black male slaves as primarily physical and promiscuous. The rhetoric of self-sacrifice also links Tom to republican martyrdom: the popular representation of America as a nation founded by men willing to die for liberty. He and fellow slave George, though dramatically different in temperament, embody the virtues associated with George Washington and other revolutionary heroes memorialized in print and popular culture throughout the nineteenth century. They value family over money, have an inherent love of freedom, and will risk their own well-being rather than sacrifice their morals.[34] Tom's struggle with murderous slave-owner Simon Legree combined with Stowe's comparison of Legree to the devil and Tom's martyrlike death all evoke a holy war. But Tom's heroic battle is not for martial or economic power. It is for the souls of US citizens.

Eliza's husband, George, is no martyr. He is nonetheless a hero molded in a form recognizable from discursive representations of the American Revolution: he will risk all for freedom and to protect his family. On the run from a brutal master, George encounters his former factory boss. Despite feeling sympathy for George, Mr. Wilson admonishes him for breaking the law. Like Mrs. Bird and Tom, George argues that if the law does not reflect virtuous principles, he is not ethically bound to obey it. While Mrs. Bird and Tom insist on following God's law rather than man's, George adheres to his belief in the rights of man and freedom, echoing sentiments of the revolutionary fathers: "I'll fight for my liberty to the last breath I breathe. You say your fathers did it; if it was right for them, it is right for me!"[35] After escaping to Canada, George and Eliza establish a loving home for their children before traveling to Europe for George's education and eventually to Liberia to work as missionaries. They find the courage to escape slavery and start anew in their commitment to freedom, a moral affiliation that necessitated civil disobedience. Like Senator Bird, George and Eliza's most virtuous acts occur when they transgress official-sphere propriety. Sending George and Eliza to Liberia instead of ending the novel, for example, with their involvement in American antislavery efforts defangs the revolutionary message of Stowe's novel in important ways but does not diminish the author's critique of political corruption and promotion of alternative values.[36]

Stowe calls into question the capacity of a commercial republic to offer citizens an affiliative identity that increases rather than corrupts virtue. In this way it adds force to the notion that political counterpublics are a better space for the growth and practice of civic virtue. Stowe argues that the United States has ceded ethical ground and leading citizens have forgotten the values of its founding fathers. Citizens with economic and political power excuse themselves from moral behavior while politically marginalized subalterns maintain their commitment to virtue in both private and public. Gillian Brown, Elizabeth Ammons, and Jane Tompkins locate the revolutionary element of *Uncle Tom's Cabin* in the novel's suggestion that for society to improve, patriarchal institutions must give way to matriarchal ethics.[37] This radical undercurrent goes beyond simply protesting the passage of a single unjust law such as the Fugitive Slave Act. It calls for a dramatic ideological shift within the national conscience and the cultural unconscious. An equally radical message, one that impacts all sociopolitically marginalized citizens, is evident in Stowe's portrayal of a transnational civic virtue that emerges through conviction to an ideal, and the identification of this virtue with acts of civil disobedience. This form of virtue bridges private and public life; it is an emotional commitment to an idea, accomplished through autonomous self-governance and manifested in the construction of new political communities. For citizens in the sociopolitical margins, a civic identity limited by affiliation to national identity disempowers and constricts subjectivity. A civic virtue defined by commitment to personal ideals offers full civic subjectivity to these marginalized groups and locates hope for the nation's future in their ranks.

Patriotic Aporia: Antislavery and White Nationalism in Sarah Josepha Hale's *Northwood*

Harriet Beecher Stowe was roundly condemned by antiabolitionists for the content of her novel and for having the audacity to engage in politics. Jonathan R. Thompson raged against the nerve of "diaper diplomatists and wet-nurse politicians" in New England, who heeded not the biblical injunction, "Let the woman learn in silence with all subjection."[38] Despite Stowe's own efforts to follow gender decorum by leaving the public speaking to others, even acceding this role to male relatives during her British book tour, her participation in a politically driven print counterpublic was still for many a step too far. The US ambassador to England equated Stowe's abolitionist fiction to the most infamous treachery of the revolutionary era: "Is she a citizen of the United States? Judging from the pertinacity with which she applies her talents to undermine the Constitution and degrade the character of her country, she is far worthier of repudiation and banishment than ever was Arnold or Burr. Genius does not always choose patriotism for a companion."[39] This comment typifies representation of abolitionists as anti-American traitors whose speech must be both socially and legally constrained. Conservative commentators then and now represent reform efforts as political. while vocal supporters of existing laws and power structures escape this categorization, appearing instead as neutral. The speech of women, slaves, and other marginalized citizens is only political and therefore problematic if it fails to celebrate the prevailing social and political structures that disempower them. Attacks on private virtue and personal identities are levied to discredit their politics and silence their dissent. Celebrated patriot and author Sarah Josepha Hale participated in this effort.

A few months after *Uncle Tom's Cabin* was published, Hale revised

Northwood, her 1826 antislavery novel, and began work on another novel that could be seen as part of the anti-Tom literary movement, *Liberia*. Though *Liberia* is more often discussed by critics, my focus is on *Northwood*, a novel deeply invested in the relationship between private and public virtue.[40] Biographical memorialization of Sarah Josepha Hale and much of the critical conversation about her part in nineteenth-century American literature focus on her forty-year editorship at *Godey's Lady's Book*, her role as advocate for women's education, and her enduring contributions to popular culture. Ann Douglas calls Hale "the most important arbiter of feminine opinion of her day."[41] *Godey's* tacitly avoided political commentary but offered women readers guidance on all things cultural, and Hale wielded her public stature beyond the magazine's pages.[42] Her successful campaign to make Thanksgiving a national holiday lasted for seventeen years, and she headed efforts to erect the Bunker Hill memorial. The dominant and leading purpose of Hale's literary and social work was to promote national unity, necessary for America to realize its Christian imperial destiny.

Understanding this facet of Hale's work is essential to grasping the seemingly contradictory messages within *Northwood*. It was considered one of the first American antislavery novels when it was published in 1827, though there is only one scene in which slaves make more than a metaphorical or referential appearance. Hale was far less interested in slavery than on the impact of its institutional structure on white Christian Americans. The didactic focus of the original *Northwood* is the essential role free labor and equality play in the development and fortification of a virtuous US citizenry. Slavery is a problem because it creates an aristocracy: a class that stigmatizes labor, produces extreme economic inequality, and discourages the development of rational self-governance, which Hale represents as essential to public virtue.[43]

In 1852, following closely on the heels of *Uncle Tom's Cabin's* unprecedented success, Hale reissued *Northwood* with an additional chapter and a final section of journal entries. These entries, written by the model patriarch Squire Romilly, offer biblical and imperialist defenses of slavery and amplify what was a relatively subtle antiabolition message within the original book. Reading this new edition as a unified work is disorienting.

A novel that promotes equality and free labor as essential to virtue and holds the aristocratic culture of slavery accountable for fostering corruption concludes with a vehement attack on abolition and a defense of slavery. Susan M. Ryan argues that facets of Hale's ideology that appear contradictory to contemporary scholars were not so for Hale—in particular her belief in white supremacy and Christian imperialism, and her celebration of private property.[44] Though true to an extent, no mental acrobatics or historical analysis can resolve the aporia of *Northwood*. But this ideological fracture can be partially explained by the overlay of two competing notions of republican virtue. For the majority of the book, Hale represents private virtue as essential to a healthy community and sees that virtue as dependent upon free labor. But her antiabolition message requires regression to the classical notion that virtuous citizenship is primarily a matter of obedience or service to the state. For Hale, with abolitionist speech on the rise and the specter of war growing, commitment to national stability and power superseded all other commitments. The unacknowledged implication of Hale's discordant text is that in the antebellum, slave-labor-reliant US, practicing civic virtue meant the sacrifice of private virtues. In addition to this discordance, which writes corruption into the American narrative, Hale's nationalistic message is undercut by her vision of a racially homogeneous Anglo-Saxon destiny. Hale sought to reshape the demos by promoting a specific vision of civic inclusion, one that placed white Christians (even those yet to emigrate from Europe) inside the civic body while expelling all others.

Hale's indictment of the slave system, rather than an effort to eradicate slavery, serves as warning to the white men and women who constitute her vision of the demos. "The acquiring or holding property is not sin—but 'the love of money is the root of all evil,' and through the temptations thus arising from wealth, it may be all but impossible 'for a rich man to enter into the kingdom of God.' Thus the system of slavery increases the temptations to sin, and only the most resolute courage in duty and humble reliance on Divine aid can struggle on successfully against the snares of evil around the slaveholder."[45] The conflict in *Northwood* is between America's destiny, which lies in the hands of Anglo-Saxons, and the degrading powers of the South's aristocratic culture. Slavery is only problematic in Hale's worldview because it perpetuates aristocracy in America. Because of slavery, men and women in the South view labor as degrading. There is no motivation to be more educated, moral, or self-disciplined when wealth is inherited, so southern men and women who should share in the imperial destiny of their New England brethren are losing their way. The novel warmly embraces a Yankee ideal as the model of salvation: labor, duty, family, Christian benevolence, all of which are identified as qualities of the Anglo-Saxon family alone.

Hale's admonition against luxury and its counterpart vice unfolds through Sidney Romilly, whose transregional life allows Hale to offer contrasting descriptions of the northern and southern households in which he was raised. Like other sentimental fiction from this period, domestic relations propel the novel's political message. As a young man, Sidney is taken to live with his aunt Lydia and her husband, Mr. Brainard, on their plantation in South Carolina. Domesticity and family life in the South are characterized by physical and emotional vacancy, which Hale largely credits to the lost need for labor both inside and outside the home. Although the activities of their life are reported, the author describes no real relationship between Lydia and her husband, only regret and ennui. Aristocratic culture, which necessitates they move about in the world and court society's good opinion, disconnects the Brainards from one another and from the domestic space they share. While Mr. Brainard spends time gambling and socializing with friends in the city, Lydia pursues her own social pleasures or rambles listlessly about the house. Lydia was "naturally industrious; and had they been poor, the efforts to procure a livelihood would have prevented that melancholy vacuity of mind she experienced while sauntering from apartment to apartment in her splendid mansion, where nothing required her care and nothing interested her feelings."[46] Slavery thwarts Lydia's development; labor was what she needed to overcome vanity and vacuity. She has no work to give her life a sense of purpose or to emotionally attach her to the home.

Hale represents labor within and for the home as a key to domestic fulfillment and virtue. In *Manners; or, Happy Homes and Good Society all the Year Round*, Hale argues that national stability and morality depend upon the attachment of men to their homes, warning wives, "Do not . . . leave *him to spend his evenings alone.*"[47] When the home is not a working unit, men will go into the world to seek their pleasures in vice. Sidney's New Hampshire family, the Romillys, are the novel's model citizens: they labor together, live frugally, and in so doing teach their children how to lead a moral life. There are no servants in the home. The boys help their father work outside on the farm; the girls help their mother maintain a clean, tastefully decorated, and highly organized home. In a comparative reading of *Northwood* and Sedgwick's *Hope Leslie*, Suzanne Gosset and Barbara Anne Bardes observe the essential but highly subordinate role played by women in Hale's work and the part their submissive domesticity plays in promoting national interests: "Virtue is seen as developing sequentially through the three levels of community organization—family, village, and country—and the basis of this virtue is family instruction. Women at home are essential to the whole system."[48] Mrs. Romilly is an ideal wife and mother in this regard. Her efforts to nurture domestic life contrast sharply with Lydia's listless wandering. Whereas the Brainards' slaves take care of everything, Mrs. Romilly eschews all domestic help. "No domestics appeared, and none seemed necessary. Love, warm hearted love, supplied the place of cold duty; and the labor of preparing the entertainment was, to Mrs. Romilly, a pleasure which she would not have relinquished to have been made an empress."[49] Mrs. Romilly's freely given labor contrasts both with the inactive life of southern aristocrats and the soulless labor of slaves. Slaves do not labor for love, and work itself is degraded by its association with subjugation and punishment. Hale provides no images or descriptions of slave labor, but this implication runs throughout her didactic commentary on the virtue of labor as an expression of love and a source of familial unity.

Hale imagines an ideal community organized around free labor and general economic equality, but suggests this is only possible for white Christians. Free labor encourages the cultivation of virtues in most of *Northwood*'s residents. Two exceptions to this rule are Deacon Jones and Ephraim Skinner. Jones, whose niece Annie Redington will become Sidney's wife, is self-righteous and greedy. He adopts an abolitionist stance solely because he enjoys feeling morally superior to his neighbors (he is the only abolitionist character in the novel). Through Deacon Jones, Hale acknowledges that not all men are going to be naturally benevolent and generous like Squire Romilly, but Deacon Jones's unchristian instincts are tempered by his membership in a community of equals. Squire Romilly explains why New England life inspires men to cultivate their character: "Character is very essential . . . public opinion, when rightly directed, exercises a censorship more appalling to vice than any punishment a tyrant could inflict." In a community of equals, reputation affects standing, so it is in Deacon Jones's best interest to act in a way the community will deem virtuous. After building a great hall, Mr. Jones offers it to the town as a meeting space for religious and community gatherings. He is soon elected a deacon, "a station he had long coveted, and no doubt often sincerely prayed for, but which, had he not made himself useful to his brethren, might not have been so readily or spontaneously granted him."[50] A community of equals rewards men like Squire Romilly, who are respected for their virtues, and neutralizes the potential harm from men like Deacon Jones. Mr. Jones controls his baser instincts to save his reputation, which is based on public-sphere expectations regarding virtue.

Deacon Jones, however, is not the true villain of *Northwood*. That appellation belongs to Ephraim Skinner, storekeeper and moneylender. Skinner's inclusion clarifies the racial dimension of Hale's ideal community: social pressure between equals only works in a racially homogeneous community because non-Anglo-Saxons are naturally inferior. Deacon Jones can be saved and integrated into the civic body; Skinner cannot. Reminiscent of Cooper's plundering band of Skinners, Ephraim Skinner fleeces virtuous neighbors, taking advantage of their hardships to drive them into debt so he can seize their property. "The love of money—not merely the root of evil, remember, but of all evil—has taken such entire possession of his heart and soul, that it deadens or destroys every kindly feeling of his nature. There is no passion so engrossing as the love of money." Why does the pressure to balance self-interest with social needs in this homogeneous community not compel Skinner to temper his vice as it does Deacon Jones? Though Hale avoids explicit mention of his religion, the most obvious answer is that Skinner is Jewish.

Ephraim is a Hebrew name meaning "double fruitfulness." When Skinner is introduced to the reader, the honest and virtuous Dr. Perkins describes him as "a merchant, a moneylender, and a miser."[51] Skinner's role as a legitimate shopkeeper fades behind anti-Semitic descriptions of wealth gained through dishonesty and manipulation. In the end, Skinner is imprisoned for fraud. Skinner's expulsion from the ideal republican community fortifies the racial dimension of Hale's vision of the United States' moral value to the world. America's national mission is to become a site for Christian, Anglo-Saxon (white) civilization. The presence of Jews and blacks endangers this destiny.

Northwood was originally an antislavery novel that espoused the value of labor. The 1852 expansion repositions the novel to promote America's white imperialist mission. Antebellum readers are urged to secure the unity of their Anglo-Saxon leaders as the standard-bearers of a burgeoning Christian empire. In a new chapter, Mr. Frankford, Sidney's English friend, serves as the bridge between Anglo-Saxons in America and those in the Old World. He attends Sunday sermon with a cynical attitude toward the United States, but the minister's sincerity and rational arguments win him over. Using strong language, the minister represents England as an empire on the precipice of "decay," exhibiting the "imbecility of age." "Will not," he asks his listeners, "luxury enervate her spirit as it did that of Greece? Will not the extension of her empire weaken her power, as it did that of Rome?" However, there is hope and comfort. After the "nations of Europe" band together and take England's power, "then will America remember her; and here shall her exiles and her fugitives find a refuge and a home. Here, mingling with a people descended from the same stock, speaking the same language, inheriting the same passion for liberty, and worshipping the same God—brothers and Christians—they will feel that they yet have a country." Though in 1852 the nation was diverse on all these fronts—racial, linguistic, ideological, and religious—Hale sees and represents white, English-speaking, republican Christians as inside the demos. All others are inadequate, even threatening. As Amy Kaplan cogently argues, "The rhetorics of Manifest Destiny and domesticity share a vocabulary that turns imperial conquest into spiritual regeneration in order to efface internal conflict or external resistance."[52] Hale promotes commitment to the goal of national unity but sees the possibility for unity as strictly limited to a racially and religiously homogeneous population—liberty in *Northwood* is not a cohering ideological commitment but a quality belonging only to the white race. Abolitionist writing openly challenged US law and politics. Hale represented herself as a true patriot for defending the political status quo despite her belief that slavery posed a direct threat to private and public virtue. Her white transnational affiliation both contradicts and supersedes her promotion of free labor, liberty, and civic virtue.

CONCLUSION

Martineau, Stowe, and Hale demonstrate the extent to which modern civic virtue is defined by individual commitment to beliefs and ideals rather than service to the nation. Even Hale, whose antiabolitionist message explicitly urges patriotic commitment to law and order above all else, undercuts herself by passionately promoting white (trans)nationalism. All three writers sought to influence the shape of the American demos. Hale, a mainstream arbiter of popular culture, endorsed a constricted public sphere. Although she believed white Christian women had an important role to play in the nation, all other politically marginalized groups are represented as destabilizing threats. Martineau and Stowe promoted increased participation from the margins by representing diverse members of the abolitionist community as superior in virtue to the politicians and businessmen who uphold laws based on economic interest or political pragmatism.

Abolitionism exemplifies the importance of public-sphere access for political subalterns. It also captures how often discourse about politics and protest was not strictly about the cause itself, but about regulating who should or should not be allowed to speak. In chapter 4 of *A Narrative of the Life of Frederick Douglass*, Frederick Douglass describes incidents of brutality against slaves, outrageous acts of violence and murder. Douglass is particularly incensed by the lack of consequences for perpetrators. A coldblooded overseer, Mr. Gore, shoots a slave named Demby in the head at pointblank range because after being whipped,

Demby sought relief in a creek and did not emerge quickly enough. Demby's murder only increased Mr. Gore's reputation as a slave breaker. "His horrid crime was not even submitted to judicial investigation. It was committed in the presence of slaves, and they of course could not institute a suit, nor testify against him; and thus the guilty perpetrator of one of the bloodiest and most foul murders goes unwhipped of justice, and uncensored by the community in which he lives."[53] After critiquing the failure of official-sphere powers to hear slaves' testimony, Douglass highlights the complicity of all community members who sanction Mr. Gore's actions by ignoring his crime.

The final section of Douglass's narrative adds to this critique of public complicity by decrying the collusion of southern Christian ministers with men in power who commit or authorize such violence. "The dealer gives his bloodstained gold to support the pulpit, and the pulpit, in return, covers his infernal business with the garb of Christianity."[54] The church and more generally the community itself are extrajudicial sites of censure that can and should step in to assert standards of justice and virtue in a culture that denies specific citizens' legal recourse. When the public sphere (where such condemnation should occur) fails, progress can feel impossible and transformative justice entirely out of reach. Though for some the modern public sphere is a space of reputation-management, Douglass and other abolitionists who sought to shame complicit citizens show that the failure or success of social pressure has important sociopolitical implications. How virtue is defined, what acts are honored or censured, who is seen and represented as fully human and capable of moral autonomy: all these delineations affect the capacity of the public sphere to serve as a check-and-balance on injustice and to continue being a productive site for democratization in government and law. Counterpublic community participants seeking political justice assert their autonomy, their right to membership in the demos, their right to a civic identity, and most fundamentally, their right to be heard.

Conclusion

Private Virtue, Counterpublics,
and Political Autonomy

THE US BECAME A NATION-STATE just as the modern bourgeois public sphere and counterpublics were gaining traction, exploring their capacity to incite change and encouraging democratic participation by politically subjugated citizens. As mercantile capitalism altered social dynamics and cultural power began shifting to the middle classes, economic philosophers and politically engaged writers promoted the importance of private virtue. Tracing the impact of mercantilism and the growth of a market economy in the eighteenth century, Pocock argues that "the universe of real property and personal autonomy now seemed to belong to a historic past; new and dynamic forces, of government, commerce, and war, presented a universe which was effectively superseding the old but condemned the individual to inhabit a realm of fantasy, passion, and amour-propre." He goes on to say that this shift destroyed the cultural paradigms on which civic virtue rested, raising the specter of inescapable corruption. While that cultural shift did challenge classic notions of civic subjectivity and virtue, contained within this instability were seeds of liberation, avenues for carving out new political spaces within the nation for citizens historically denied full legal or civic identities. As private virtue gained stature, women transmuted their domestic role to a national one, claiming the authority and moral autonomy previously reserved for property-owning men. Literature of the late eighteenth century demonstrates a growing push to democratize civic virtue by locating it within domestic spaces inhabited by average citizens rather than the public spaces of aristocratic politicians or war heroes. In 1792 Barbauld asserted, "The first principle, therefore, we must lay down is, that we are to submit our public conduct to the same rules by which we are to regulate our private actions."[1] Barbauld represented public virtue as deeply intertwined with private identity and encouraged all citizens to understand themselves as morally implicated in and responsible for national politics and policies. Then and now, conservatives have reasserted classical notions of republican virtue to discredit counterpublic activism, but civic virtue has been increasingly defined by a host of factors not anchored to martial service, obedience to the state, or property-based autonomy.

This challenge to the civic humanist tradition was enabled by the growth of a print public sphere. The mainstream public sphere described by Habermas—the cafés and clubs where newspapers circulated, the ships that carried pamphlets about trade and politics across the sea, and all the other spaces predominantly inhabited or controlled by enfranchised men—provided the bourgeoisie a social and textual space for political deliberation. While expressing concern for its functionality, Habermas reasserts the importance of this sphere in his later work: "Thus, on the republican conception, the political public sphere and its base, civil society, acquire a strategic significance. Together they are supposed to secure the integrative power and autonomy of the communicative practice of the citizens." Habermas's continued idealization of rational-critical norms, his emphasis on "subjectless modes of communication," ascribes classical humanist baggage to a public sphere that developed while civic virtue's terms were under siege. Nancy Fraser, Michael Warner, and Lauren Berlant have gone far to address this contradiction and limitation in their work on counterpublics and intimate publics.[2] By highlighting the collision between civic virtue's discursive evolution and the emergence of counterpublics, I continue this effort. I also demonstrate that the public sphere's purpose and spirit, its ability to "secure the integrative power and autonomy" of citizens and realize its "strategic significance" is located most redolently in counterpublics.

Counterpublics offer ideals-driven intra- and international communal identities and provide forums in which marginalized and oppressed citizens can gather to challenge the state. These public-sphere debates can revise the identity-based boundaries that leave some within the territorial borders of a nation outside its civic body, leaving the promise of democracy only partially fulfilled. British radical Harriet Martineau wrote about the poetic spirit of early America: the relative equality and faith in man she witnessed in the western states gave her hope for the future of democracy. French philosopher Jacques Ranciere calls the democratic man a "poetic being, a being capable of embracing a distance between words and things which is not deception, not trickery, but humanity; a being capable of embracing the unreality of representation. A poetic virtue, then, and a virtue grounded in trust." Michael Warner contends that "a public is poetic world making." While perhaps inimical to preindustrial ideologies of republican virtue, "passion, fantasy, and *amour-propre*" are no enemy to democratization.[3] Passion drives politically marginalized citizens to fight for publicity, and imagination allows those individuals to understand themselves as connected to others within textually mediated, transnational publics. In regards to amour propre, when your subjectivity is denied validity, when your right to speak is challenged, a little vanity can be generative rather than destructive. Political counterpublics represent a living, breathing, discursively and practically powerful democratic force. They are broad-based communities that grow organically, though not without volition, from a shared desire to institute sociopolitical change. They have the power to revive important questions about democracy and the state, assert or challenge social norms, and expand civic involvement by creating affective political agency. Life in the public sphere and the formation of counterpublics continue to impact individual and communal identity formation while playing a pivotal role in reshaping democracy.

The Contemporary Public Sphere

Habermas, Pocock, and Arendt all raise concerns about how a market-driven public sphere affects individual subjectivity. Although these concerns are particularly justified in the media-saturated contemporary US, the relationship between reputation management and political or social justice is not always inimical. Frederick Douglass's narrative captures the capacity of even regional variations in social norms to either sanction or inhibit oppressive regimes. On plantations in the South, neither the church nor the general community considered violence against slaves shameful. In Baltimore—closer to free states, densely populated, with non-slave-owners always nearby—the standards were different. "A city slave is almost a freeman, compared with a slave on the plantation. He is much better fed and clothed, and enjoys privileges altogether unknown to the slave on the plantation. There is a vestige of decency, a sense of shame, that does much to curb and check those outbreaks of atrocious cruelty so commonly enacted upon the plantation. . . . Few are willing to incur the odium attaching to the reputation of being a cruel master." The time Douglass spent in Baltimore provided him with opportunities the Deep South did not. Learning how to read (against his owners' wishes) and experiencing a modicum of freedom altered Douglass's self-understanding and played an integral role in his developing knowledge of liberation movements, including abolitionism. Katherine Henry aptly observes, "Exclusion from the public realm . . . meant that one was not only unprotected, subject to physical violence, but also silenced, prevented from representing oneself discursively."[4] After escaping slavery, Douglass dedicated his life to altering public opinion through live speeches and print publications. Asserting his civic subjectivity, Douglass helped shape the nineteenth-century abolitionist counterpublic, insisting on the right of a former slave to participate in deliberative democracy. The ultimate goal of abolitionism was the legal end to slavery. Publicity meant to alter norms was an essential component of the struggle.

Today's antiracist activists demonstrate an equally thoughtful understanding of the collusion between social norms, public-sphere dialogue, and political change. The diffuse discourse communities enabled by the internet provide contemporary proponents of racial justice with an ever-ready means of communicating to their publics. Warner contends that a public is defined by continuing print and reception as well as by the existence of an audience that includes strangers. Both these qualities are more readily producible today. The Black Lives Matter movement and the widespread activism it has inspired exemplify the power of a visible counterpublic to facilitate new dialogue and public action. Black Lives Matter is a "Black-centered political will and movement building project." Its purpose is to "organize and build local power to intervene in violence inflicted on Black communities by the state and vigilantes." The movement began after George Zimmerman was acquitted of charges in the murder of Trayvon Martin, a teenage boy Zimmerman shot while on neighborhood patrol. When the state sanctioned this killing by not holding Zimmerman legally accountable, Alicia Garza, Patrisse Culors, and Opal Tometi created Black Lives Matter. The movement is designed to amplify the voices of black activists who have been sidelined within dominant liberation movements, whose public leaders are often heterosexual men. In this sense it represents a radical counterpublic, one that builds on and challenges other antiracist counterpublics that have reproduced forms of domination and silencing. The movement recognizes the relationships between public discourse surrounding race, the actions of private citizens in public spaces, and the continuance of state-sanctioned violence against black citizens. The importance of participatory space and political will are written into the movement's philosophy.[5]

Counterpublics, by reshaping discourse, have the capacity to close the *differend*, the victimization that occurs when one party cannot present their wrong because the opposition's idiom, not theirs, creates the framework of understanding.[6] Before the Black Lives Matter movement drew attention to contemporary patterns of violence incited and sanctioned by racism, mainstream media coverage rarely discussed these events as evidence of a widespread and systemic issue. Efforts to publicize racially motivated violence and to show patterns of injustice changed the idiom. Through social media and the press, antiracism activists have described a multitude of ways (not always involving immediate physical violence) that black bodies are subjected to threatening public scrutiny. It is hard to imagine these conversations manifesting before the protests and discussions inspired by Black Lives Matter, a movement that supports Warner's contention that "identity politics . . . seems to many people a way of overcoming both the denial of public existence that is so often the form of domination and the incoherence of the experience that domination creates, an experience that often feels more like invisibility than like the kind of privacy you value."[7] Barbecue Becky called the police on a family cooking out in a public park. Other African Americans have been reported to authorities for engaging in peaceful public activities. A young girl selling water during a gay pride parade in San Francisco was threatened with police action if she did not produce a "permit"; the cops were called on a twelve-year-old boy providing lawn mowing services; and multiple stories of black residents being harassed at their community pools have come to light. This is only a sampling of the private-citizen patrolling captured on video. Conversations around these events are rife with frustration: America's legal system offers no recourse to those being harassed. Weaponizing the emergency 911 number is a tool for public-sphere constriction. Criminalizing the existence of minorities helps push them inside their homes, sending a clear signal that not everyone has the right to a public subjectivity. Robin Lakoff contends that "hate speech in any form both presupposes and recreates a narrative in its very utterance: the story of who has had power over whom, and how that power is maintained, and what will happen to anyone who challenges that power . . . so word and action merge in narrative meaning-making, allowing covert control because the story need not be told in so many (or any) words. The status quo is maintained. Control of the story is control of history."[8] White men and women confidently call police because a narrative history proves they will be believed and their target will not.

Activists who draw attention to the resonances between contemporary public sphere policing and the country's long history of African American oppression are working to disrupt this narrative. Like nineteenth-century abolitionists, they push for social condemnation as a springboard for political change. The perpetrators of racially motivated phone calls and explicit hate speech caught on camera have largely avoided state-based punishment, facing instead counterpublic-driven private consequences: social shaming and the economic hardship of lost work. The ability of activists to mobilize the public exemplifies the public sphere's capacity to perpetuate domination of oppressed citizens or to discourage marginalizing behaviors by creating extrajudicial consequences. In response to efforts to make minorities fear public life, activists call for private-sector punishments to reassert antiracist social norms. Since Black Lives

Matter began speaking, writing, and organizing against police brutality, the antiracist political counterpublic has grown exponentially, demonstrating the extent to which "the idea of a public is motivating, not simply instrumental."[9] While political theorists may bemoan the loss of privacy, growth of reputation management, and seeming irrationality that mark contemporary public life, counterpublic movements like Black Lives Matter and Me Too have demonstrated the political public sphere's continuing importance for those fighting to build a more inclusive and participatory democracy.

Notes

INTRODUCTION

1. Shelley Burtt, *Virtue Transformed: Political Argument in England, 1688–1740* (New York: Cambridge University Press, 1992), 4.

2. Nancy Fraser, "Rethinking the Public Sphere: A Contribution to the Critique of Actually Existing Democracy," *Social Text* 25/26 (1990): 56–80.

3. Fraser, "Rethinking the Public Sphere"; Jürgen Habermas, *The Inclusion of the Other: Studies in Political Theory*, ed. Ciaran Cronin and Pablo De Greiff (Cambridge: MIT Press, 1998). Habermas has expanded and revised his analysis of the contemporary public sphere, particularly in *The Inclusion of the Other*. Although Habermas maintains that the public sphere is threatened by the mass welfare state, this work reiterates the important role it plays when operating independently of the state.

4. Elizabeth Maddock Dillon, *The Gender of Freedom: Fictions of Liberalism and the Literary Public Sphere* (Stanford, CA: Stanford University Press, 2004); Sarah Knott, *Sensibility and the American Revolution* (Chapel Hill: University of North Carolina Press, 2009). These two books are especially relevant in American studies.

5. Jürgen Habermas, *The Structural Transformation of the Public Sphere: An Inquiry into a Category of Bourgeois Society*, trans. Thomas Burger with the assistance of Frederick Lawrence (Cambridge: MIT Press, 1991), 56.

6. John Locke, *Two Treatises on Government and a Letter Concerning Toleration* (London: Churchill, 1689–90; repr., ed. Ian Shapiro, New Haven: Yale University Press, 2003).

7. Michael Warner, *Publics and Counterpublics* (New York: Zone Books, 2002).

8. Lauren Berlant, *The Female Complaint: The Unfinished Business of Sentimentality in American Culture* (Durham, NC: Duke University Press, 2008); Lauren Berlant, *The Queen of America Goes to Washington City: Essays on Sex and Citizenship* (Durham, NC: Duke University Press, 1997); Anne Phillips, *Engendering Democracy* (University Park: Pennsylvania State University Press,

1991); Katherine Henry, *Liberalism and the Culture of Security: The Nineteenth-Century Rhetoric of Reform* (Tuscaloosa: University of Alabama Press, 2011).

9. Warner, *Publics and Counterpublics*, 40.

10. Berlant, *The Queen of America Goes to Washington City*, 11.

11. Phillips, *Engendering Democracy*, 25.

12. Berlant, *The Female Complaint*, 3.

13. John Kane, *The Politics of Moral Capital* (New York: Cambridge University Press, 2001); Christopher Leslie Brown, *Moral Capital: Foundations of British Abolitionism* (Chapel Hill: University of North Carolina Press, 2006). Though this concept belongs to Kane, my use was more significantly influenced by Brown's exploration of moral capital in abolitionist discourse.

14. Cassandra Santiago and Doug Criss, "An Activist, a Little Girl and the Heartbreaking Origin of 'Me Too,'" CNN online, October 17, 2017; "More Than 12M 'Me Too' Facebook Posts, Comments, Reactions in 24 Hours," CBS News online, October 17, 2017; Richard Blaug, *Democracy, Real and Ideal: Discourse Ethics and Radical Politics* (Albany: State University of New York Press, 1999), 138.

15. Seyla Benhabib, *Another Cosmopolitanism* (Oxford: Oxford University Press, 2006), 67, emphasis in the original. Benhabib discusses the French protest against restrictions on religious clothing, led by young women who wanted to regain the right to wear their hijabs at school.

16. Julia Raifman, Ellen Moscoe, S. Bryn Austin, and Margaret McConnell, "Difference-in-Differences Analysis of the Association between State Same-Sex Marriage Policies and Adolescent Suicide Attempts," *JAMA Pediatrics* 171, no. 4 (2017): 350–56.

17. Judith Butler, *Undoing Gender* (New York: Routledge, 2004), 7.

18. Markman Ellis, *The Politics of Sensibility: Race, Gender, and Commerce in the Sentimental Novel* (New York: Cambridge University Press, 1996), 23; Amy Kaplan, *The Anarchy of Empire in the Making of U.S. Culture* (Cambridge, MA: Harvard University Press, 2002), 18; Jane P. Tompkins, *Sensational Designs: The Cultural Work of American Fiction, 1790–1860* (New York: Oxford University Press, 1985), 10–18, xvi.

19. Laura M. Stevens, "Transatlanticism Now," *American Literary History* 16, no. 1 (2004): 93–102; Susan Manning and Andrew Taylor, eds., *Transatlantic Literary Studies: A Reader* (Baltimore: Johns Hopkins University Press, 2007); Eve Tavor Bannett and Susan Manning, eds., *Transatlantic Literary Studies, 1660–1830* (New York: Cambridge University Press, 2012).

20. Stevens, "Transatlanticism Now," 94.

21. Manning and Taylor, *Transatlantic Literary Studies*, 7.

22. Harriet Martineau, *Society in America* (New York: Saunders & Otley, 1837; repr., New York: Anchor Books, 1962), 73; Harriet Martineau, "The Martyr Age of the United States," *Westminster Review* (December 1838; repr., New York: Arno Press, 1969).

CHAPTER ONE

1. Anna Laetitia Barbauld, *Sins of Government, Sins of the Nation; or, a Discourse for the Fast, Appointed on April 19, 1793. By a Volunteer* (London: J. Johnson, 1793; repr., Ann Arbor: University of Michigan Library, 2007), 33, ECCO-TCP.

2. Emma Major, "Ithuriel's Spear: Barbauld, Sermons, and Citizens, 1789–93," *Journal for Eighteenth-Century Studies* 41, no. 2 (2018): 257–72. Major discusses Barbauld's work and motivation. She argues that *Sins of Government, Sins of the Nation* was a type of sermon, a logical genre for eighteenth-century women who were looking to validate participation in the political public sphere.

3. Lance Banning, "Some Second Thoughts on 'Virtue' and the Course of Revolutionary Thinking," in *Conceptual Change and the Constitution*, ed. Terence Ball and J. G. A. Pocock (Lawrence: University Press of Kansas, 1988), 199. In his analysis of American revolutionaries, Banning argues that revolutionary ideals were distinguished by the belief that "individuals, who would inevitably assert their personal demands when making political decisions, might mistake the public good; but none could possibly escape involvement in the public fate, and none should ever forget that the public fate would be his own." Barbauld's work demonstrates that this attitude can be traced, at least in part, to British counterpublic activism.

4. Rachel Trethewey, "Lady Defender of the Revolution: Barbauld among the British Radicals," in *Anna Letitia Barbauld: New Perspectives*, ed. William McCarthy and Olivia Murphy (Lanham, MD: Bucknell University Press, 2014), 138. Trethewey demonstrates that although Barbauld is frequently represented as a political moderate and proper Christian woman, during her lifetime she was considered a radical. That was particularly true in the 1790s, when Barbauld published *Sins of Government* and "Civic Sermons," both of which encouraged the lower and middle classes to become more involved in politics. Horace Walpole labeled her "that virago Barbauld" and lumped her in with other troublesome female writers, the "Amazonian allies headed by Kate Macaulay." The Amazonian accusation suggests an improper desire to engage in statesmanship and battle.

5. Warner, *Publics and Counterpublics*, 39; Phillips, *Engendering Democracy,*

24. Scholars have pointed out the extent to which, while privacy may have diminished, the "private citizen" became central to notions of governance at liberalism's inception. Warner argues that this element of Locke's work was fundamental to the redefinition of public and private life. Phillips points out that for Hobbes and Locke the importance of property ownership in defining political status informed theorization of the government's role as a safeguard for an individual's private life from external threats. In this way, liberalism granted the "private individual" primacy.

6. Hannah Arendt, *The Human Condition: A Study of the Central Dilemmas Facing Modern Man* (New York: Doubleday, 1959), 61, 63. Arendt's perspective on mobile property aligns with J. G. A. Pocock's assertion that a speculative market economy deeply impacted the relationship between private and public virtue as well as identity formation more generally: "The dissolution of [the private] realm into the social may most conveniently be watched in the progressing transformation of immobile into mobile property until eventually the distinction between property and wealth . . . loses all significance."

7. Henry, *Liberalism and the Culture of Security*, 13.

8. Habermas, *The Structural Transformation of the Public Sphere*, 4; Arendt, *The Human Condition*, 65.

9. This gap in Arendt's and Habermas's work has been exposed by scholars seeking to re-center embodied existence in theorizing public-sphere politics; see Phillips, *Engendering Democracy*; Warner, *Publics and Counterpublics*; and Henry, *Liberalism and the Culture of Security*.

10. Habermas, *The Structural Transformation of the Public Sphere*, 19.

11. Fraser, "Rethinking the Public Sphere," 56–80. For a discussion of the role such erasure played in meeting the needs of male heterosocial culture during this period, see G. J. Barker-Benfield, *The Culture of Sensibility: Sex and Society in Eighteenth-Century Britain* (Chicago: University of Chicago Press, 1992), 53. Feminist scholars, particularly in studies of early American culture, have taken aim at the absence of women in Habermas's delineation of the print public sphere. See Nina Baym, *American Women Writers and the Work of History* (New Brunswick, NJ: Rutgers University Press, 1995); Cathy N. Davidson's edited collection *No More Separate Spheres! A Next Wave American Studies Reader* (Durham, NC: Duke University Press, 2002); Shirley Samuels, *Romances of the Republic: Women, the Family, and Violence in the Literature of the Early American Nation* (New York: Oxford University Press, 1996); Anne K. Mellor, *Mothers of the Nation: Women's Political Writing in England, 1780–1830* (Bloomington: Indiana University Press, 2000); and Dillon, *The Gender of Freedom*.

12. For a more thorough history of British abolitionism, see Judith Jennings, *The Business of Abolishing the British Slave Trade* (London: Routledge, 1997).

13. For discussion of this issue, see David Morse, *The Age of Virtue: British Culture from the Restoration to Romanticism* (New York: Palgrave, 2000), 2; James Sambrook, *The Eighteenth Century: The Intellectual and Cultural Context of English Literature, 1700–1789* (New York: Longman, 1986), 69; Burtt, *Virtue Transformed*, 15–16; and J. G. A. Pocock, *The Machiavellian Moment: Florentine Political Thought and the Atlantic Republican Tradition* (Princeton: Princeton University Press, 1975), 425–26, all of whom identify the revolution, constitution, and resultant political shifts collectively as the inception point for eighteenth-century moral philosophy.

14. Pocock, *The Machiavellian Moment*, 426.

15. Brett D. Wilson, "Hannah More's Slavery and James Thomson's Liberty: Fond Links, Mad Liberty, and Unfeeling Bondage," in *Invoking Slavery in the Eighteenth-Century British Imagination*, ed. Srividhya Swaminathan and Adam R. Beach (Surrey, Eng.: Ashgate Press, 2013), 118. Wilson describes the mistrust in both government and a "monied interest" that grew out of the South Sea bubble, a company whose failure, brought about by dishonest stockjobbing, caused bankruptcies across the nation.

16. James Sambrook, *The Eighteenth Century*, 69. Sambrook provides a summary of events to argue that confidence in the nation grew, particularly during the early and mid-eighteenth century, due to "a real economic strength" that grew out of expanded commerce, finance, and the beginning stages of the industrial revolution.

17. Athol Fitzgibbons, *Adam Smith's System of Liberty, Wealth, and Virtue: The Moral and Political Foundations of* The Wealth of Nations (New York: Clarendon Press, 1995), 23. Kaye makes a parallel argument in his introduction to *The Fable of the Bees; or, Private Vices, Publick Benefits (1732 edition)* (Oxford: Clarendon Press, 1924), xcvii.

18. Jerry Z. Muller, *The Mind and the Market: Capitalism in Modern European Thought* (New York: Knopf, 2002), 57.

19. Maxine Berg, *Luxury and Pleasure in Eighteenth-Century Britain* (New York: Oxford University Press, 2005), 22.

20. David Hume, "Of Refinement in the Arts," in *Essays, Moral, Political, and Literary*, ed. Eugene F. Miller (London: Millar, Kincaid, & Donaldson, 1889; repr., Indianapolis: Liberty Fund, 1987), Online Library of Liberty; Adam Smith, *An Inquiry into the Nature and Causes of the Wealth of Nations* (London: W. Strahan & T. Cadell), 1776; repr., ed. Jim Manis, Hazelton: Pennsylvania State University, 2005), http://www.rrojasdatabank.info/adamsmith/wealthp1.pdf.

See, in particular, Hume's "Of Refinement" (originally titled "Of Luxury").
In *Wealth of Nations*, Smith represents "opulence" as an essential step in the
progress that occurs as societies move from subsistence agriculture to urban
republics.

21. Quoted in Berg, *Luxury and Pleasure in Eighteenth-Century Britain*, 22.

22. This conversation was not limited to British philosophers. A number
of scholars have explored concepts of luxury and virtue in France during this
period. Rousseau, Diderot, and Montesquieu were significant voices in this
continental debate although their work is outside the scope of this book. For
historically and geographically expansive scholarship, see Pocock, *The Machia-*
vellian Moment; Muller, *The Mind and the Market*, wherein he revisits the work
of British, Dutch, and French writers; and John Shovlin, *The Political Economy*
of Virtue: Luxury, Patriotism, and the Origins of the French Revolution (Ithaca, NY:
Cornell University Press, 2006) for coverage of this debate in France.

23. Bernard Mandeville, *The Fable of the Bees: or, Private Vices, Publick Bene-*
fits (1732 edition). With a Commentary Critical, Historical, and Explanatory by F.B.
Kaye, Vol. 1 (Oxford: Clarendon Press, 1924), 324.

24. Anthony Ashley Cooper, Earl of Shaftesbury, *Characteristicks of Men,*
Manners, Opinions, Times, vol. 2 (1737), ed. Douglas Den Uyl (Indianapolis:
Liberty Fund, 2001), 31, Online Library of Liberty.

25. Because of Shaftsbury's emphasis on benevolence rather than masculine martial virtues, scholars have argued that female writers over the next
hundred years were drawn to his philosophy. For an extended consideration of
this relationship, see Karen O'Brien, *Women and Enlightenment in Eighteenth-*
Century Britain (New York: Cambridge University Press, 2009).

26. Sambrook, *The Eighteenth Century*, 55.

27. Kaye, Introduction to *The Fable of the Bees*, lxx.

28. Quoted in Burtt, *Virtue Transformed*, 128.

29. Mandeville, *The Fable of the Bees*, 12–13.

30. Mandeville, *The Fable of the Bees*, 7.

31. Mandeville, *The Fable of the Bees*, 34–35.

32. Barbauld, *Sins of Government, Sins of the Nation*, 396.

33. One procommerce argument made by both Mandeville and Hume is
that the least wealthy classes in England enjoy a better general quality of life than
the wealthiest citizens in ancient societies or those in contemporary societies
who do not engage in manufacturing or extensive trade.

34. Sambrook, *The Eighteenth Century*, 56.

35. Hume, "Of Refinement in the Arts," 271.

36. Hume, "Of Refinement in the Arts," 273–74.

37. David Hume, "Of Commerce," in *Essays, Moral, Political, and Literary*, ed. Eugene F. Miller (London: Millar, Kincaid, and Donaldson, 1889; repr., Indianapolis: Liberty Fund, 1987), II.I.17, Online Library of Liberty.

38. Hume, "Of Refinement in the Arts," 277.

39. Adam Smith, *The Theory of Moral Sentiments* (London: A. Millar, A. Kincaid, & J. Bell, 1759; repr., New York: Classic House Books, 2009), 51.

40. Smith, *The Theory of Moral Sentiments*, 57.

41. Smith, *The Theory of Moral Sentiments*, 61.

42. Muller, *The Mind and the Market*, 75. Muller discusses Adam Smith's favorable view of the moral impact of the free market in *The Wealth of Nations* (1776), which has everything to do with a leveling of the classes. Per Smith, the free market stamps out obsequiousness and rewards honesty and fair dealing.

43. Pocock, *The Machiavellian Moment*, 462–64.

44. Pocock, *The Machiavellian Moment*, 464.

45. Pocock, *The Machiavellian Moment*, 483–87.

46. Burtt, *Virtue Transformed*, 7.

47. Smith, *The Theory of Moral Sentiments*, 252.

48. Smith, *The Theory of Moral Sentiments*, 257.

49. Jane Rendall, "Virtue and Commerce: Women in the Making of Adam Smith's Political Economy," in *Women in Western Political Philosophy: Kant to Nietzsche*, ed. Ellen Kennedy and Susan Mendus (New York: St. Martin's Press, 1987), 45.

50. Smith, *The Theory of Moral Sentiments*, 257.

51. Rendall, "Virtue and Commerce," 45.

52. Brown, *Moral Capital*, 27, 153, 450; Karen E. Weyler, *Empowering Words: Outsiders and Authorship in Early America* (Athens: University of Georgia Press, 2013), 5–6.

53. John Kane, *The Politics of Moral Capital* (New York: Cambridge University Press, 2001), 7.

54. Ranciere, Jacques. *Dissensus: On Politics and Aesthetics*, trans. Steven Corcoran (New York: Continuum, 2010), 70, 32, 20, 19.

55. Dana Harrington, "Gender, Commerce, and the Transformation of Virtue in Eighteenth-Century Britain," *Rhetoric Society Quarterly* 31, no. 3 (2001): 33–52; Linda Kerber, "The Republican Mother: Women and the Enlightenment—An American Perspective," *American Quarterly* 28, no. 2 (1976): 187–205; Linda Kerber, *Women of the Republic: Intellect and Ideology in Revolutionary America* (Chapel Hill: University of North Carolina Press, 1980). Harrington describes these eighteenth-century female authors as progenitors of "Republican Motherhood," a phrase coined in 1976 by Kerber in "The Republican

Mother" and further developed in *Women of the Republic: Intellect and Ideology in Revolutionary America* (Chapel Hill: University of North Carolina Press), 1980.

56. Harrington, "Gender, Commerce, and the Transformation of Virtue in Eighteenth-Century Britain," 45.

57. Linda Colley, *Britons: Forging the Nation, 1701–1837* (New Haven: Yale University Press, 1992), 250.

58. See Moira Ferguson, *Subject to Others: British Women Writers and Colonial Slavery, 1670–1834* (New York: Routledge, 1992), and Mellor, *Mothers of the Nation.*

59. Catherine Ingrassia, "Contesting 'Home' in Eighteenth-Century Women's Verse," in *Home and Nation in British Literature from the English to the French Revolutions*, ed. A. D. Cousins and Geoffrey Payne (New York: Cambridge University Press, 2015), 154–68; Paula R. Backscheider, *Eighteenth-Century Women Poets and Their Poetry: Inventing Agency, Inventing Genre* (Baltimore: Johns Hopkins University Press, 2005), 8; Tricia Lootens, *The Political Poetess: Victorian Femininity, Race, and the Legacy of Separate Spheres* (Princeton: Princeton University Press, 2017); Berlant, *The Female Complaint*, 3. Ingrassia, Backscheider, and Lootens offer scholarly analyses of poetry that demonstrate the extent to which during the 1780s and 1790s, abolitionist literature was already a genre in which women explored social and political issues. Ingrassia discusses abolition and antiwar poetry, and citing in particular the work of Aphra Behn, Backscheider argues that "the women poets of the 1790s had inherited and brought to maturity the potential for power in the public sphere." Both Backschedier's and Lootens' texts describe the communal aspect of poetry, which was shared in book clubs and through lending libraries and provided material for public performance. In this way, writing, reading, and performing poetry challenged the boundaries between private emotion and public life. These smaller social connections made by female poets built what Berlant calls in *The Female Complaint* an "intimate public." Working within generic conventions helps intimate publics build an audience and feel like part of a shared project, and in the process "provides an affective confirmation of the idea of a shared confirming imaginary in advance of inhabiting a material world in which that feeling can actually be lived." The growth in popular female poetry over the course of the eighteenth century provided the foundation for a broader-reaching, politically bound community of abolitionist poets, each of whom utilized conventional tropes within their poetry while simultaneously challenging the social conventions that circumscribed their political role as women.

60. Ann Yearsley, *A Poem on the Inhumanity of the Slave Trade* (London: G. G. J. & J. Robinson, 1788), http://www.brycchancarey.com/slavery/yearsley1.htm;

Maria Falconar and Harriet Falconar, *Poems on Slavery* (London: Egertons, Murray, & Johnson, 1788), http://www.brycchancarey.com/slavery /falconar.htm; Hannah More, *Slavery: A Poem* (London: T. Cadell, 1788), http://www.brycchancarey.com/slavery/morepoems.htm; Anna Laetitia Barbauld, *Epistle to William Wilberforce, Esq. on the Rejection of the Bill for Abolishing the Slave Trade* (London: J. Johnson, 1791), http://www.brycchancarey.com /slavery/barbauld1.htm; Mary Birkett Card, *A Poem on the African Slave Trade: Addressed to Her Own Sex* (Dublin: J. Jones, 1792), http://www.brycchancarey. com/slavery/mbc1.htm. Yearsley, the Falconars, and More all published in 1788. Barbauld's poem came in 1791; Card's, in 1792.

61. Kenneth Morgan, *Slavery, Atlantic Trade, and the British Economy, 1660–1800* (New York: Cambridge University Press, 2000), 157. Morgan describes the explosion of propaganda during the late 1780s and early 1790s, which included poems, pamphlets, and petitions. It is estimated that "between 1787 and 1792 petitions against the slave trade were signed by 1.5 million out of 12 million people in Britain." Morgan credits the widespread popular participation in this debate to its moral appeal and to the involvement of women in the movement. Anne K. Mellor, "The Female Poet and the Poetess: Two Traditions of British Women's Poetry, 1780–1830," *Studies in Romanticism* 36, no. 2 (1997): 264.

62. More's and Yearsley's religious sentiments were complex and fluctuating. For analysis of this issue, see Monica Smith Hart, "Protest and Performance: Ann Yearsley's Poems on Several Occasions," in *The Working-Class Intellectual in Eighteenth- and Nineteenth-Century Britain* (Surrey, Eng.: Ashgate, 2009), 49–66.

63. For example, see Tompkins, *Sensational Designs*; Ann Douglas, *The Feminization of American Culture*, 1st ed. (New York: Knopf, 1977); and Dillon, *The Gender of Freedom*.

64. More, *Slavery, a Poem*, 6. In a similar vein, More compares Africans to Romans during their imperial heyday, equally proud and passionate. This similarity aligns Africans with a classical martial form of virtue, while suggesting that England has evolved past this imperial model.

65. Yearsley, *A Poem on the Inhumanity of the Slave Trade*, 6.

66. Ferguson, *Subject to Others*, 146. See also Srividhya Swaminathan and Adam R. Beach, eds., *Invoking Slavery in the Eighteenth-Century British Imagination* (Surrey, Eng.: Ashgate Press, 2013), which offers wide-ranging reflection on the use of slavery as symbol and metaphor during this period.

67. Ramesh Mallipeddi, *Spectacular Suffering: Witnessing Slavery in the Eighteenth-Century British Atlantic* (Charlottesville: University of Virginia Press, 2016), 8.

68. JoEllen DeLucia, *A Feminine Enlightenment: British Women Writers and the Philosophy of Progress, 1759–1820* (Edinburgh: Edinburgh University Press), 2015, 10. DeLucia seeks to dismantle the generalized notion that Enlightenment thought consistently valued reason and denigrated "feminine" sentimentalism. Smith's *Theory of Moral Sentiments* is at the center of DeLucia's argument, showing the extent to which both Smith's work and literature during this period "privileged emotion above reason and saw progress as a move toward a more feminine world marked by heightened emotional states."

69. More, *Slavery, a Poem*, lines 251–54.

70. Falconar and Falconar, *Poems on Slavery*, 22.

71. Barbauld, *Epistle to William Wilberforce, Esq.*, 11, 9.

72. Barbauld, *Epistle to William Wilberforce, Esq.*, 12.

73. Falconar and Falconar, *Poems on Slavery*; Card, *A Poem on the African Slave Trade*; Yearsley, *A Poem on the Inhumanity of the Slave Trade*. The Falconars mention both Albion and Britannia, who evoke a symbolic, historically based, and morally purposeful national identity. Card speaks to Albion while Yearsley refers to Britannia throughout her poem. Britannia in particular was a redolent image for female activists as she was frequently deployed both in print and in art to represent political conflict and imperial activities. See Wilson, "Hannah More's Slavery and James Thomson's Liberty," 223–25, for an example of political art featuring Britannia.

74. Card, *A Poem on the African Slave Trade*, 3.

75. Charlotte Sussman, *Consuming Anxieties: Consumer Protest, Gender, and British Slavery, 1713–1833* (Stanford, CA: Stanford University Press, 2000). Sussman discusses the many valences of rhetoric around consumption, from protests against slave-produced goods, particularly sugar, to the rhetoric of contagion often evoked by abolitionist work.

76. Yearsley, *A Poem on the Inhumanity of the Slave Trade*, 27, emphasis in original.

77. Barbauld, *Epistle to William Wilberforce, Esq.*, 14.

78. John Aikin and Anna Laetitia Barbauld, *Evenings at Home; or, the Juvenile Budget Opened: Consisting of a Variety of Miscellaneous Pieces . . .* vol. 5 (London: J. Johnson, 96; repr., Ann Arbor, MI: Text Creation Partnership, 2009), 85, 86, ECCO-TCP.

CHAPTER TWO

1. Richard Blaug, *Democracy, Real and Ideal: Discourse Ethics and Radical Politics* (Albany: State University of New York Press, 1999), 138.

2. Major, "Ithuriel's Spear," 258. Major argues that the sermon, which would have gone by many other names (*discourse*, *appeal*, or *address*) in the eighteenth century, was a significant component of the growing print public sphere. In the 1790s, for every page of fiction, eight pages of sermon were published.

3. "Debate in the Commons on the King's Proclamation against Seditious Writings," in *The Parliamentary History of England from the Earliest Period to the Year 1803*, vol. 29 (London: T. C. Hansard, 1817), 1476–90, Google Books. In 1792 the king delivered a proclamation that exemplified the backlash against this democratic outbreak. In it, he and the Privy Council did "strictly charge and command all our magistrates in and throughout our kingdom of Great Britain, that they do make diligent inquiry in order to discover the authors and printers of such wicked and seditious writings as aforesaid . . . that they do, in their several and respective stations, take the most immediate and effectual care to suppress and prevent all riots, tumults, and other disorders, which may be attempted to be raised or made by any person or persons, which on whatever pretext they may be grounded, are not only contrary to the law, but dangerous to the most important interests of the kingdom."

4. The government jailed many publishers throughout the 1790s, including Barbauld's own, Joseph Johnson. In 1793 alone at least eight publishers were tried for sedition. For the specifics of Johnson's case, see Leslie F. Chard II, "Joseph Johnson in the 1790s," *Wordsworth Circle* 33, no. 3 (2002): 95–100.

5. Wil M. Verhoeven, "Gilbert Imlay and the Triangular Trade," *William and Mary Quarterly*, 3rd ser., 63, no. 4 (2006): 827; John Seelye, "The Jacobin Mode in Early American Fiction: Gilbert Imlay's *The Emigrants*," *Early American Literature* 22, no. 2 (1987): 204–12. Verhoeven characterizes *The Emigrants* as "America's first frontier novel and only Jacobin novel." John Seelye's essay focuses primarily on establishing the Jacobin credentials of Imlay's work.

6. Pocock, *The Machiavellian Moment*, 540.

7. For a fuller exploration of Rousseauian ideas in Imlay's work, see Wil M. Verhoeven and Amanda Gilroy, introduction to *The Emigrants* (New York: Penguin, 1998), ix–xliv.

8. Knott, *Sensibility and the American Revolution*, 44. Knott provides a succinct description of liberal ideology in early American literature, tied most notably to the philosophies of John Locke and John Stuart Mill: Fiction from the revolutionary era explores "the common themes of the pursuit of individual self-interest and the sanctity of contract, in a world of natural liberty restrained only by a minimal state." While Imlay's novel does not expressly promote the pursuit of self-interest, it is implied by his protagonists' founding their own closed community rather than working toward broader social change. The final

element in Knott's list accurately reflects Imlay's work as the state seemingly disappears in *The Emigrants*' separatist utopia.

9. Oliver Farrar Emerson, "Notes on Gilbert Imlay, Early American Writer," *PMLA: Publications of the Modern Language Association of America* 39, no. 2 (1924): 406–39; Wil. M. Verhoeven, *Americomania and the French Revolution Debate in Britain, 1789–1802* (New York: Cambridge University Press, 2013); Joseph F. Bartolomeo, "No Place like Home: The Uses of America in 1790s British Fiction," *Yearbook of English Studies* 46 (2016). For contemporary reviews of Imlay's work that demonstrate its public impact, see Emerson, "Notes on Gilbert Imlay." In *Americomania*, Verhoeven discusses the reason for this impact: a deep interest in America during the revolutionary era, both as political experiment and symbol of renewal. Bartolomeo demonstrated how Imlay's work was part of an arc in utopic literature, which in the 1790s responded to anxiety over commercialism and explored the possibilities of agrarian republicanism, making America a potent tool for critiques or celebrations of home.

10. Verhoeven and Gilroy, introduction to *The Emigrants*, xiv.

11. Verhoeven, "Gilbert Imlay and the Triangular Trade," 827–42.

12. Quoted in Verhoeven, "Gilbert Imlay and the Triangular Trade," 838.

13. Andrew R. L. Cayton, *Love in the Time of Revolution: Transatlantic Literary Radicalism and Historical Change, 1793–1818* (Chapel Hill: University of North Carolina Press, 2013), 64.

14. Wollstonecraft moved to France in late 1792 with prorevolutionary ideals. In 1793 she and Gilbert Imlay became romantically involved. Through both his work for the government and his relationship with Wollstonecraft, Imlay had access to political writers and expatriated English intellectuals, exposing him to various perspectives on social and political revolution.

15. Rosalie Murphy Baum, "*The Emigrants*: An American Utopia in Kentucky," *Journal of Kentucky Studies* 23 (2006): 155. The disjunction between Imlay's life and the values espoused in his novels explains the inconsistencies identified by Baum, who attributes the discordant messages in *The Emigrants* to conflict between four eighteenth-century discourses: the "philosophy of sensibility, views of Pantisocrats, radical feminism (on love and marriage), and style conventions of the sentimental novel." Baum's article captures the continuing appeal of Imlay's work for sociopolitical study (if not for the general public; *florid* does not quite do Imlay's prose justice).

16. The audience for both of Imlay's texts was decidedly European. A US edition of *The Emigrants* was not published until 1964. See Verhoeven and Gilroy, introduction to *The Emigrants*, xxxi.

17. Verhoeven, *Americomania*, 1. Verhoeven explicates the effect America

had, as a symbol of what was possible, on the "dawning of political liberty and social equality in modern British society."

18. Based on the content of contemporary journal reviews, didactic commentary on free love likely kept *The Emigrants* from finding a broader reading public.

19. See Verhoeven's *Americomania* for sustained consideration of the relationship between the French and American Revolutions and British modernity.

20. Gilbert Imlay, *A Topographical Description of the Western Territory of North America; Containing a Succinct Account of Its Soil, Climate, Natural History, Population, Agriculture, Manners, and Customs*, 3rd ed. (London: J. Debrett, 1797; repr., New York: A. M. Kelly, 1969), vi.

21. Cayton, *Love in the Time of Revolution*, 59.

22. Imlay, *Topographical Description*, xii.

23. Tilar J. Mazzeo, "The Impossibility of Being Anglo-American: The Rhetoric of Emigration and Transatlanticism in British Romantic Culture, 1791–1833," *European Romantic Review* 16, no. 1 (2005): 62–63. Wil Verhoeven's focus on the radical aspect of Imlay's writing has influenced scholarly discussion, sometimes eliding the broader appeal written into this agrarian utopianism. For example, in an article focused on English romantic writers' rejection of transatlantic self-identification, Mazzeo focused solely on the radical element. Mazzeo specifically discusses the social and political issues that informed the pantisocratic emigration scheme: "Plans for pantisocracy were informed by a lively public debate surrounding the issues of emigration, national wealth, agriculture, commerce, and population growth." Mazzeo's list of key issues echoes eighteenth-century discourse on luxury and virtue, which would have resonated for a broad reading population, not solely in radical circles. While Imlay may have been filtering radical physiocratic philosophy through his work, his concurrent participation in this active and diffuse public conversation invites a reconsideration, or at least a broadening of accepted understanding, of his intended audience.

24. Imlay, *Topographical Description*, 552.

25. John Ashworth, *"Agrarians" and "Aristocrats": Party Political Ideology in the United States, 1837–1846*, 1st ed. (New York: Cambridge University Press, 1987), 28. Ashworth's comment on democratic rhetoric during this era reflects a similar level of vague idealization of agrarianism, which may have influenced Imlay's utopic vision: "The democrats envisaged an essentially undifferentiated society in which the farmer laboured almost in isolation for his wealth and then sold his produce in a series of straightforward, undemanding operations."

26. Corey Robin, *The Reactionary Mind: Conservatism from Edmund Burke*

to Sarah Palin (Oxford: Oxford University Press, 2013), 29. Robin argues that profeudalistic nostalgia is a cornerstone of conservative rhetoric: "There is no better way to exercise power than to defend it against an enemy from below. Counterrevolution, in other words, is one of the ways in which the conservative makes feudalism seem fresh and medievalism modern." Interestingly, he describes this appeal as a "reactionary utopia," which aptly describes Imlay's purportedly Jacobin work.

27. Verhoeven, "Gilbert Imlay and the Triangular Trade," 830.

28. Imlay, *Topographical Description*, 168.

29. Imlay, *Topographical Description*, 200. Imlay offers a strongly worded critique of manufacturing, crediting it with the power to corrupt men by giving them access to luxuries, destabilizing the community, and negatively impacting the overall morality of the people: "I detest the manufacturing system; observing the salacious prosperity it induces, its instability, and its evil effect on the happiness and the morals of the bulk of the people. You must on this system have a large portion of the people converted into mere machines, ignorant, debauched, and brutal, that the surplus value of their labour of 12 or 14 hours a day, may go into the pockets and supply the luxurious of the rich, commercial, and manufacturing capitalists."

30. Imlay, *Topographical Description*, 169.

31. John Funchion, "Reading Less Littorally: Kentucky and the Translocal Imagination in the Atlantic World," *Early American Literature* 48, no. 1 (2013): 65, https://doi.org/10.1353/eal.2013.0015. Funchion describes Imlay's Bellefont as a "heterotopia," a term borrowed from Foucault: "Unlike national spaces, heterotopias are marked with temporal discontinuities and ruptures. They can preserve a fossilized past awaiting recovery or bear the promise of a better future, as they often did in the transatlantic writing about Kentucky." Kentucky was particularly ripe for such imaginaries because of its precarious political status. Though it was a territory of Virginia, which allowed men like Imlay to buy and resell its land, it remained a target of French and Spanish imperial interest during this period. Funchion argues this status added to Kentucky's international appeal, marking it as a local site with transatlantic significance.

32. Imlay, *Topographical Description*, 168.

33. Gilbert Imlay, *The Emigrants* (1793; repr., New York: Penguin, 1998), 53.

34. Imlay, *The Emigrants*, 30.

35. Imlay, *The Emigrants*, 224.

36. Janet Todd, *Death and the Maidens: Fanny Wollstonecraft and the Shelley Circle* (Berkeley, CA: Counterpoint, 2007), 31–32. Todd's biography quotes one of Imlay's letters, written in response to a request from friend Joseph Johnson

and Fanny Imlay's stepfather, William Godwin, that Imlay follow through on his promise to provide Fanny with financial support. In this letter, Imlay "begged Johnson not to humiliate him further." As Todd aptly observes, "There was much concerning his image here, nothing about his daughter." Todd's take on Imlay differs from Andrew Cayton's, but both demonstrate the extent to which Imlay was engaged in constant reputation-management for the sake of financial survival and personal gain.

37. Imlay, *The Emigrants*, 225, emphasis in original.

38. Imlay, *The Emigrants*, 165.

39. Imlay, *The Emigrants*, 255–56.

40. The romantic representation of an "Anglo-Saxon" America was common throughout the long nineteenth century, in what might now be termed a racial dog whistle: coded terminology that directly appealed to belief in white supremacy. In *Eighteenth-Century Women Poets and Their Poetry*, Paula Backscheider discusses the racial element of abolitionist poetry that nostalgically represents premodern Britain and Anglo-Saxon identity. The same can be seen in *The Emigrants*, though as Juliet Shields points out in *Nation and Migration: The Making of British Atlantic Literature, 1765–1835* (Oxford: Oxford University Press, 2016), it is the ancient "Briton" whom Imlay most potently romanticizes.

41. Imlay, *The Emigrants*, 236–37.

42. Gordon S. Wood, *The Creation of the American Republic, 1776–1787* (Chapel Hill: University of North Carolina Press, 1969), 35–38. Physical impotency suggests a political impotency that endangers the republic. Wood argues that the dissipation of citizens in a republic was believed by many to be the precursor of tyranny because it kept them from actively policing those in power. According to Wood, rhetoric of English society that painted it as effeminate, debauched, and addicted to luxury was used to fortify a proindependence stance.

43. Imlay, *The Emigrants*, 80. For an analysis focused on the family romance and the role chivalry plays in Imlay's utopia, see Juliet Shields, "Genuine Sentiments and Gendered Liberties: Migration and Marriage in Gilbert Imlay's *The Emigrants*," in *Atlantic Worlds in the Long Eighteenth Century: Seduction and Sentiment*, ed. Toni Bowers and Tita Chico (New York: Palgrave Macmillan, 2012), 33–47.

44. Nicole Pohl and Brenda Tooley, eds., *Gender and Utopia in the Eighteenth Century: Essays in English and French Utopian Writing* (Burlington, VT: Ashgate, 2007), 8; John Mac Kilgore, "John Lithgow's Real Utopia and the Anticapitalist Romance of the Early Republic," *Early American Literature* 54, no. 1 (2019): 116; Cayton, *Love in the Time of Revolution*; Shields, "Genuine

Sentiments and Gendered Liberties." Exploring eighteenth-century gender ideology in utopic literature, Pohl and Tooley summarize the essay findings to show that no matter the gender of the writer, "some of these utopian narratives qualified or contested masculinist discourses, whereas others endorsed these discourses by buying into essentialist categories of gender." Clearly influenced by Rousseau's idealization of natural gender identities, Imlay's text offers an essentializing portrayal that despite its origin in radical circles promotes and romanticizes separate spheres. Discussing *The Emigrants*, Kilgore argues that Imlay's novel "challenges the status quo model of republican sentimentalism . . . in order to position women as autonomous and equal public-private actors" (116). The chivalric model here, however, is defined by female dependency and masculine leadership. Andrew Cayton and Juliet Shields further demonstrate the masculinist element of Imlay's utopia.

45. In keeping with his promotion of free love and less stringent divorce laws, Imlay's model of chivalry shifts one important aspect of the medieval romance, wherein masculine aspiration was driven by a love that could never be consummated. Written into the scenes between Capt. Arl-ton and Caroline and into the novel as a whole is the promise of sexual fulfillment. See Seelye, "The Jacobin Mode in Early American Fiction," for an extended analysis of erotics in the novel.

46. Imlay, *The Emigrants*, 247.

47. Baum, "*The Emigrants*: An American Utopia in Kentucky," 163.

48. Karsten H. Piep, "Separatist Nationalism in Gilbert Imlay's *The Emigrants*," *CLCWeb: Comparative Literature and Culture* 6, no. 4 (2004): 4, https://doi.org/10.7771/1481-4374.1247. Piep describes *The Emigrants* as "an early example of a form of *separatist nationalism*" that imagines the nation as a collection of distinct communities rather than a "cohesive, solid, homogenous America." Claiming Bellefont reflects dissident nationalism, Piep ignores its homogeneity.

49. Imlay, *Topographical Description*, 75, 76.

Chapter Three

1. James Fenimore Cooper, *The American Democrat* (Cooperstown, NY: Elihu Phinney, 1838; repr., New York: Barnes & Noble, 2004), 126.

2. John P. McWilliams Jr., *Political Justice in a Republic: James Fenimore Cooper's America* (Berkeley: University of California Press, 1972), 42. McWilliams locates similar sentiments in *Notions of the Americans: Picked Up by a Traveling Bachelor*, vol. 2 (Philadelphia: Carey, Lea, & Blanchard, 1828. Nabu Public

Domain Reprints), https://archive.org/stream/cihm_50256?ref=ol#mode/2up. In Cooper's discussion of the revolutionary era, encomiums on figures like George Washington and General Lafayette reveal the extent to which "Cooper associates republican virtue with the patrician gentleman who is a disinterested upholder of liberty. . . . Such men exemplify for Cooper the great values of individual disinterest and social privacy."

3. The majority of scholars who have engaged in comparative analyses of Cooper and Sedgwick discuss the authors' frontier romances, *The Last of the Mohicans* and *Hope Leslie*. See Carolyn L. Karcher, "Catharine Maria Sedgwick in Literary History," in *Catharine Maria Sedgwick: Critical Perspectives*, ed. Lucinda L. Damon-Bach and Victoria Clements (Boston: Northeastern University Press, 2003), 5–16; Susan K. Harris, "The Limits of Authority: Catharine Maria Sedgwick and the Politics of Resistance," in *Catharine Maria Sedgwick: Critical Perspectives*, ed. Lucinda L. Damon-Bach and Victoria Clements, 5–16 (Boston: Northeastern University Press, 2003); Amanda Emerson, "History, Memory, and the Echoes of Equivalence in Catharine Maria Sedgwick's *Hope Leslie*," *Legacy* 24, no. 1 (2007): 24–49; and Susanne Opfermann, "Lydia Maria Child, James Fenimore Cooper, and Catharine Maria Sedgwick: A Dialogue on Race, Culture, and Gender," in *Soft Canons: American Women Writers and Masculine Tradition*, ed. Karen L. Kilcup (Iowa City: University of Iowa Press, 1999), 27–47. For a comparative analysis of gender, race, and republicanism in *The Last of the Mohicans* and *Hope Leslie*, see Shirley Samuels, "Women, Blood, and Contract," *American Literary History* 20, 1–2 (2008): 57–75; and Andy Doolen, "Blood, Republicanism, and the Return of George Washington: A Response to Shirley Samuels," *American Literary History* 20, nos. 1/2 (2008): 76–82.

4. Gerald J. Kennedy, *Strange Nation: Literary Nationalism and Cultural Conflict in the Age of Poe* (Oxford: Oxford University Press, 2016), 31; Joe Shapiro, *The Illiberal Imagination: Class and the Rise of the U.S. Novel* (Charlottesville: University of Virginia Press, 2017), 2. In *Novels in the Time of Democratic Writing: The American Example* (Philadelphia: University of Pennsylvania Press, 2018), Nancy Armstrong and Leonard Tennenhouse argue that prior to the 1830s a plethora of lesser-read American novels represented private property as "incorrigibly antisocial" and celebrated freedom of circulation between interlinked social networks. James Fenimore Cooper's *The Spy: A Tale of the Neutral Ground* (New York: Wiley, 1821; repr., New York: Penguin, 1997) takes the opposite position but reflects the connection described by Armstrong and Tennenhouse between perspectives of private property and social mobility. Cooper celebrates property while painting mobility and fluid social networks as dangerously destabilizing.

5. Samuels, *Romances of the Republic*, 17.

6. Dillon, *The Gender of Freedom*, 20, 21.

7. Smith. *The Theory of Moral Sentiments*, 21.

8. Heinz Ickstadt, "Instructing the American Democrat: Cooper and the Concept of Popular Fiction in Jacksonian America," in *James Fenimore Cooper: New Critical Essays*, ed. Robert Clark (Harrisonburg, VA: Vision Publishers, 1985), 23.

9. Allan M. Axelrad, "James Fenimore Cooper, American English, and the Signification of *Aristocracy* in a Republic," *Literature in the Early American Republic* 6 (2014): 158.

10. McWilliams, *Political Justice in a Republic*, 47; Waples, *The Whig Myth of James Fenimore Cooper*, 56.

11. Shapiro, *The Illiberal Imagination*, 12.

12. Cooper, *The American Democrat*, 121.

13. Some scholars have traced efforts by Cooper and his peers to discursively manage US republican identity to the political upheavals of the early antebellum period. The Jacksonian era saw the rise of a new political party (i.e., the modern Democratic Party) and eventually the election of Andrew Jackson, the first US president without a purely aristocratic pedigree. Jackson's cultural impact was partially in what his political ascendency symbolized: the ability of men with middling origins to gain significant political power. His election was both fearfully and triumphantly credited to "the people" by politicians and the press. For a broad introduction to the Jacksonian era, see Arthur Schlesinger, *The Age of Jackson* (Boston: Little, Brown, and Co., 1945). For a discussion of Jackson and patriotic nostalgia in literature of the 1820s–1850s, see Alfred F. Young, *The Shoemaker and the Tea Party: Memory and American Revolution* (Boston: Beacon Press, 1999); and Michael Kammen, *A Season of Youth: The American Revolution and the Historical Imagination* (New York: Knopf, 1978).

14. Cooper, *The American Democrat*, 39.

15. Cooper, *The American Democrat*, 21, 134.

16. Corey Robin, *The Reactionary Mind: Conservatism from Edmund Burke to Sarah Palin* (Oxford: Oxford University Press, 2013), 10.

17. Dorothy Waples, *The Whig Myth of James Fenimore Cooper* (Hamden, CT: Archon, 1968); John P. McWilliams Jr. "Cooper and the Conservative Democrat," *American Quarterly* 22 (1970): 665–77; Shapiro, *The Illiberal Imagination*. Few scholars (relative to the size of Cooper's critical canon) have meted out *The Spy's* political valences in relationship to Cooper's explicit critique of populism in *The American Democrat*, though Waples, McWilliams, and Shapiro all touch on these texts in discussions of Cooper's political ideology.

18. Emily Miller Budick, *Fiction and Historical Consciousness: The American Romance Tradition* (New Haven: Yale University Press, 1989), 11.

19. Kennedy, *Strange Nation*, 233.

20. Quoted in Robert Clark, "Rewriting Revolution: Cooper's War of Independence," in *James Fenimore Cooper: New Critical Essays*, ed. Robert Clark (Harrisonburg, VA: Vision Publishers, 1985), 200.

21. Cooper, *The Spy*, 210, 258.

22. Cooper, *The Spy*, 94, 391.

23. Cooper, *The Spy*, 192, 163.

24. Cooper, *The American Democrat*, 77; Cooper, *The Spy*, 41.

25. Cooper, *The Spy*, 363, 69, 49; Dillon, *The Gender of Freedom*, 11.

26. Clark, "Rewriting Revolution," 187–205. Clark analyzes *The Spy* and *Wyandotte*, Cooper's later revolutionary war novel, arguing that Cooper participates in a conservative effort to deny the extralegal origins of the United States. Citizens who desire stability and value private property, Clark contends, must repudiate revolutionary violence and construct a gentry-centric origin story.

27. Cooper, *The Spy*, 185, 226.

28. For works focused on Birch, see Tremaine McDowell, "The Identity of Harvey Birch," *American Literature: A Journal of Literary History, Criticism, and Bibliography* 2, no. 2 (May 1930): 111–20; and Jack Kligerman, "Notes on Cooper's Debt to John Jay," *American Literature: A Journal of Literary History, Criticism, and Bibliography* 41, no. 3 (November 1969): 415–19. For a take on Birch in relation to Cooper's effort to downplay revolutionary rhetoric, see James Franklin Beard, "Cooper and the Revolutionary Mythos," *Early American Literature* 11, no. 1 (1976): 84–104. For articles that continue this tradition while exploring the theme of masking, see James Beard Franklin, "Cooper and the Revolutionary Mythos," *Early American Literature* 11, no. 1 (1976): 84–104; and Hugh Crawford, "Cooper's Spy and the Theater of Honor," *American Literature* 63, no. 3 (September 1991): 405–19.

29. Cooper, *The Spy*, 397.

30. Karcher, "Catharine Maria Sedgwick in Literary History," 12.

31. Baym, *American Women Writers*, 8.

32. Catharine Maria Sedgwick, *The Linwoods; or, "Sixty Years Since" in America* (New York: Harper & Brothers, 1835; repr., Hanover, NH: University Press of New England, 2002), 360; Catharine Maria Sedgwick, *The Power of Her Sympathy: The Autobiography and Journal of Catharine Maria Sedgwick*, ed. Mary Kelley (Boston: Massachusetts Historical Society, 1993), 46. In a series of letters written to her niece, Sedgwick tells the story of her family and childhood.

While her emigrant ancestors hailed from prominent and landed families, they did not sustain the wealth with which they emigrated. This ostensible misfortune, Sedgwick assures her niece, was a substantial blessing: "The wise man's prayer has been granted to us; we have enjoyed fully the advantage and felicity of being neither rich nor poor!"

33. Sedgwick, *The Power of Her Sympathy*, 64, 360.

34. Sedgwick, *The Linwoods*, 143.

35. Sedgwick, *The Linwoods*, 200.

36. Maria Karafilis, "Catherine Maria Sedgwick's *Hope Leslie*: The Crisis between Ethical Political Action and U.S. Literary Nationalism in the New Republic," *American Transcendental Quarterly* 12, no. 4 (1998): 331.

37. Philip Gould, *Covenant and Republic: Historical Romance and the Politics of Puritanism* (New York: Cambridge University Press, 1996), 114.

38. Sedgwick, *The Linwoods*, 58.

39. Sedgwick, *The Linwoods*, 102–3.

40. Sedgwick, *The Linwoods*, 204.

41. Linda Kerber, *Women of the Republic: Intellect and Ideology in Revolutionary America* (Chapel Hill: University of North Carolina Press, 1980), 40.

42. Emily VanDette, "'It Should Be a Family Thing': Family, Nation, and Republicanism in Catharine Maria Sedgwick's *A New England Tale* and *The Linwoods*," *ATQ: 19th Century American Literature and Culture* 19, no. 1 (2005): 71.

43. Sedgwick, *The Linwoods*, 7; Marissa Carrere, "Theorizing Democratic Feelings, Disagreement, and the Temporal Child in Catharine Maria Sedgwick's *The Linwoods*," *Legacy* 34, no. 1 (2017): 38.

44. Maria Karafilis, introduction to *The Linwoods; or, "Sixty Years Since" in America*, xi–xxxv (Hanover, NH: University Press of New England, 2002); Robert Daly, "Reading Sedgwick Now: Empathy and Ethics in Early America," *Literature in the Early American Republic* 2 (2010): 147; Charlene Avallone, "Catharine Sedgwick's White Nation-Making: Historical Fiction and *The Linwoods*," *ESQ: A Journal of the American Renaissance* 55, no. 2 (2009): 118. In Maria Karafilis's introduction to *The Linwoods*, she claims that Sedgwick "portrays white women and African Americans as sympathetic 'rebels' with legitimate political and social claims," and Robert Daly argues that *The Linwoods* "offers us an American Revolution far more multicultural and humanly complex than the conventional iconicity of her time allowed." Other scholars have challenged these readings. If multiculturalism purportedly includes racial difference, Sedgwick's novel falls short in this regard. While Rose is strongly admired by Isabella and plays an active role in rescuing Herbert Linwood from prison, Charlene Avallone points out that Rose's choice to remain in service to the Linwood

family after gaining her freedom "promise[s] that African Americans, enslaved or free, possess such limited desire for liberty and equality as to guarantee the implausibility of revolution, whether in the social or political order." In particular, Sedgwick's infantilizing portrait of a male slave, Jupiter, echoes the personally and politically demeaning rhetoric evident in *The Spy*, which Avallone aligns with *The Linwoods* in its vision of a white nationalist future. Though Cooper's and Sedgwick's political visions are not synonymous, Sedgwick's near silence on slavery in *The Linwoods* signals an unwillingness to wade into radical waters, though doing so would have better aligned with the more egalitarian and meritocratic messages of her text. Despite this silence, her promotion of autonomous political identity and mobility within subaltern political communities, including her portrayal of Rose, offers a significantly more democratic vision of the future than Cooper's work. For a critique of racial politics in the novel in addition to Avallone, see Kennedy, *Strange Nation*, 258–59.

45. Sedgwick, *The Linwoods*, 17; Sedgwick, *The Power of Her Sympathy*, 70. Rose's character, portrayed as strong-willed and intelligent, is thought to be based upon the Sedgwick family's real life servant, Elizabeth Freeman Mumbet. Sedgwick's father, lawyer Theodore Sedgwick, helped Mumbet sue for her freedom, which she won in 1780. In *The Power of Her Sympathy*, Sedgwick compares Mumbet to George Washington, two courageous and loyal Americans committed to truth.

46. Sedgwick, *The Linwoods*, 137.

47. Sedgwick, *The Linwoods*, 121.

48. Sedgwick, *The Linwoods*, 131, 132.

49. Sedgwick, *The Linwoods*, 321.

50. Carrere, "Theorizing Democratic Feelings," 47.

51. Sedgwick, *The Linwoods*, 322.

52. Sedgwick, *The Linwoods*, 63. Gould, *Covenant and Republic*. Gould offers an analysis of *Hope Leslie* that aligns with my analysis of gender and republicanism in *The Linwoods*, demonstrating ideological consistency in Sedgwick's fiction.

53. Robin, *The Reactionary Mind*, 7.

54. Cooper, *The Spy*, 7.

55. Habermas, *The Inclusion of the Other*, 207.

CHAPTER FOUR

1. Immanuel Kant, "An Answer to the Question: 'What Is Enlightenment?'" in *The Idea of the Public Sphere: A Reader*, ed. Jostein Gripsrud, Hallvard Moe,

Anders Mollander, Graham Murdock (New York: Rowan & Littlefield, 2010), 4. Kant is a clear predecessor of Emerson, whose representation of the ideal American scholar echoes Kant's definition of *enlightenment*, which he argues is the equivalent of *maturity*, defined as man's willingness to use his own reason and think for himself rather than acceding to dogma or letting social and political leaders think for him. Also central to Kant's definition is the willingness of an enlightened man to use his reason publicly: "By the public use of one's own reason I mean that use which anyone may make of it as a *man of learning* addressing the entire *reading public*" (emphasis in original). Both Kant and Emerson believed the enlightened individual should serve the public by sharing his knowledge. Both texts suggest it will require exceptional individual leaders rather than broad coalitions to propel society forward.

2. Benhabib, *Another Cosmopolitanism*, 169.

3. For an illuminating analysis of this distinction, see Dillon, *The Gender of Freedom* (2004), chap. 1.

4. My focus is the most common and broadly referenced tenets of liberalism, particularly for early Americanists. For a comprehensive discussion of variations in liberal theory, see John Rawls, *Political Liberalism*, expanded ed. (New York: Columbia University Press, 2005).

5. Habermas, *The Inclusion of the Other*, 208.

6. Benhabib, *Another Cosmopolitanism*, 33–34.

7. Most prominent abolitionists included Christian arguments alongside political points in speeches and writing: Harriet Beecher Stowe, Sojourner Truth, Lucretia Mott, and the Grimke sisters among them. Though Harriet Martineau uses some religious rhetoric, including the concept of martyrdom, she infamously converted during the course of her life from Unitarianism to Mesmerism in a rejection of formal religion.

8. There is a parallel between this method for measuring virtuous behavior and Adam Smith's strictures in *The Theory of Moral Sentiments* for becoming a moral individual. Smith describes two methods commonly used for judging one's own behavior: comparison to others, and comparison to the ideal of morality. The latter approach, Smith argues, is a more effective method for developing the moral sense. Both Smith and Martineau aim for an "objective" approach to moral judgment.

9. Deborah Anna Logan, *The Hour and the Woman: Harriet Martineau's "Somewhat Remarkable" Life* (DeKalb: Northern Illinois University Press, 2002). For a comprehensive understanding of Martineau's work, Logan's scholarship is essential. In addition to her biography of Martineau, Logan edited five collections of Martineau's writing. Martineau's own two-volume autobiography

also provides significant insight regarding her commitment to democracy and liberty: *Harriet Martineau's Autobiography* (Boston: James R. Osgood, 1877; repr., London: Virago, 1983).

10. Martineau, *Society in America*, 44.

11. Martineau, *Society in America*, 299.

12. Deborah Anna Logan, "'My Dearly-Beloved Americans': Harriet Martineau's Transatlantic Abolitionism," in *Nineteenth-Century British Travelers in the New World*, ed. Christine DeVine (Burlington, VT: Ashgate Press, 2013), 203. Much of Logan's biographical work emphasizes Martineau's commitment to freedom. In "My Dearly-Beloved Americans," Logan shares a eulogizing comment from Florence Nightingale that reflects contemporary understanding of the driving force behind so much of Martineau's writing: "She was born to be a destroyer of slavery, in whatever form, in whatever place, all over the world, wherever she saw or thought she saw it."

13. R. K. Webb, *Harriet Martineau: A Radical Victorian* (New York: Columbia University Press: 1960), 172, 165.

14. Martineau, *Society in America*, 73.

15. Logan, *The Hour and the Woman*, 196. Martineau's optimism waned after decades of abolitionist work resulted in no real political change, instead suffering significant losses, including passage of the Fugitive Slave Act in 1850 and the Dred Scott decision in 1857. In a private letter written around 1856, Martineau expressed lost faith in the cause though her public commitment did not abate: "I am unable to cheer my American friends much about their country. . . . As a republican experiment it will prove a failure: but we may help to make some salvage out of the wreck."

16. Harriet Martineau, "The Martyr Age of the United States," *The Westminster Review* (December 1838; repr., New York: Arno Press, 1969), 7.

17. Elizabeth Spelman, *Fruits of Sorrow: Framing Our Attention to Suffering* (Boston: Beacon Press, 1998), 50; Martineau, "The Martyr Age," 4.

18. Martineau, "The Martyr Age," 3; Ted Hovet Jr., "Harriet Martineau's Exceptional American Narratives: Harriet Beecher Stowe, John Brown, and the 'Redemption of Your National Soul,'" *American Studies* 48, no. 1 (2007): 72.

19. Warner, *Publics and Counterpublics*, 40–42. This example supports arguments against sociopolitical analyses that "bracket" the physical body, ignoring the embodied aspect of lived experience. While engaging in rational debate, abolitionists withstood public attacks based on their biological identities (in particular, women and African Americans were criticized for inappropriate publicity) and were physically threatened.

20. Martineau, "The Martyr Age," 54.

21. This argument echoes a critique made by the British abolitionist Anna Laetitia Barbauld in "Civic Sermons to the People" (London: Dundee, 1792), Google Books. The king and Parliament defended sedition laws that targeted radical publishers by claiming this literature threatened to foment public violence. Barbauld turns this rhetoric on its head, pointing to the 1791 Priestly Riots in Birmingham, during which so-called respectable citizens burned down the homes, businesses, and churches of religious dissenters. Martineau, *Society in America*, 116.

22. Leslie A. Fiedler, *Love and Death in the American Novel* (New York: Criterion, 1960), 264, 266; Elizabeth Ammons, "Heroines in Uncle Tom's Cabin," *American Literature* 49 (1977): 116–79 (repr., in *Critical Essays on Harriet Beecher Stowe*, ed. Elizabeth Ammons [Boston: G. K. Hall, 1980]), 157.

23. Tompkins, *Sensational Designs*, 125. Gillian Brown, *Domestic Individualism: Imagining Self in Nineteenth-Century America* (Berkeley: University of California Press, 1990); Tompkins, *Sensational Designs*; Jean Yellin Fagan, "Doing it Herself: *Uncle Tom's Cabin* and Woman's Role in the Slavery Crisis," in *New Essays on Uncle Tom's Cabin, Cambridge*, ed. Eric J. Sundquist (Cambridge: Cambridge University Press, 1986) 81–106; Lori D. Ginzberg, "Virtue and Violence: Female Ultraists and the Politics of Non-Resistance," *Quaker History* 84, no. 1 (1995): 17–25.

24. Hovet, "Harriet Martineau's Exceptional American Narratives," 70. Hovet discusses Martineau's complimentary notice of *Uncle Tom's Cabin*. Regarding Martineau's short antislavery novel *Demerara* (in *Illustrations of Political Economy*, 3rd ed. [London: Charles Fox, 1832], Online Library of Liberty), Hovet argues that "Stowe and Martineau intended the details of their fiction to be received by readers as both highly emotional *and* empirically grounded." Martineau's nonfiction writing on slavery, discussed earlier, demonstrates her efforts in this direction while Stowe's choice to publish the approximately 250-page *A Key to Uncle Tom's Cabin* in 1853 offers a factual response to critics who dismissed the novel as sentimental fantasy.

25. Although St. Claire and Shelby reinforce points I make later about corruption at centers of power, my discussion focuses on the adult characters in the novel. For discussions of the significance of children and childhood characters in *Uncle Tom's Cabin*, see Leslie Fiedler (*Love and Death in the American Novel*), Elizabeth Ammons ("Heroines in Uncle Tom's Cabin"), and Jane Tompkins (*Sensational Designs*).

26. Kenneth Hada, "The Kentucky Model. Economics, Individualism and Domesticity in *Uncle Tom's Cabin*," *Papers On Language and Literature: A Journal for Scholars and Critics of Language and Literature* 35, no. 2 (1999): 177; David S.

Reynolds, *Mightier than the Sword: Uncle Tom's Cabin and the Battle for America*, 1st ed. (New York: W. W. Norton, 2011), 70; Harriet Beecher Stowe, *Uncle Tom's Cabin* (Boston: John P. Jewett, 1852; repr., New York: Oxford World Classics, 1998), 15.

27. Stowe, *Uncle Tom's Cabin*, 8, 40.

28. Stowe, *Uncle Tom's Cabin*, 40, 138, emphasis in original.

29. Stowe, *Uncle Tom's Cabin*, 85.

30. Stowe, *Uncle Tom's Cabin*, 39; Hada, "The Kentucky Model," 184.

31. Stowe, *Uncle Tom's Cabin*, 262.

32. Brown, *Domestic Individualism*, 93. In a discussion of Dinah, the female slave who runs the Shelbys' kitchen, Brown argues that "Stowe calls for the reform of kitchens as a precondition to women's reform of the market economy."

33. Stowe, *Uncle Tom's Cabin*, 423–24.

34. Tompkins, *Sensational Designs*, 125; Mark J. Miller, *Cast Down: Abjection in America, 1700–1850* (Philadelphia: University of Pennsylvania Press, 2016), 112; Christopher Harris, *Public Lives, Private Virtues: Images of American Revolutionary War Heroes, 1782–1832* (New York: Garland, 2000). See Harris's discussion of memorialization of the founding fathers during this era, which was prevalent not just in fiction but in history texts, art, and journalism.

35. Stowe, *Uncle Tom's Cabin*, 118.

36. Thomas F. Gosset, *Uncle Tom's Cabin and American Culture* (Dallas: Southern Methodist University Press, 1985); Susan M. Ryan, "Errand into Africa: Colonization and Nation Building in Sarah J. Hale's *Liberia*," *New England Quarterly* 68, no. 4 (1995): 558–83; Miller, *Cast Down*, 9. Stowe herself later expressed regret for ending George's story in Liberia. See Gosset and Ryan for discussions of contemporary responses to this element of the text and analysis of its implications. Miller has argued that "Tom's martyrdom confirms a black presence at the heart of the Christian 'fellowship of man' but describes the U.S. civic body, including the public sphere, as fundamentally white." Miller claims that *Uncle Tom's Cabin* authorizes white women's public political speech; however, in this realm too the novel falls short of full endorsement. Female activism happens solely in domestic spaces. The promise of civic democratization in Stowe's novel emerges from her glorification of slaves, women, and dissenters who exemplify republican virtue rather than through clear endorsement of political power for the disenfranchised.

37. Brown, *Domestic Individualism*, 98; Ammons, "Heroines in Uncle Tom's Cabin," 157–60; and Tompkins, *Sensational Designs*, 145.

38. Quoted in David A. Copeland, *The Antebellum Era: Primary Documents on Events from 1820 to 1860* (Westport, CT: Greenwood, 2003), 346.

39. British book tour discussed in Reynolds, *Mightier than the Sword*, 46; Gosset, Uncle Tom's Cabin *and American Culture*, 257.

40. For an in-depth discussion of *Liberia*'s white imperialist politics, see Ryan, "Errand into Africa," and Amy Kaplan, "Manifest Domesticity," *American Literature: A Journal of Literary History, Criticism, and Bibliography* 70, no. 3 (1998): 581–606.

41. Douglas, *The Feminization of American Culture*, 51. Hope Greenberg, "*Godey's Lady's Book*: Publication History," University of Vermont, http://www.uvm.edu/~hag/godey/glbpub.html. Greenberg reports that "by 1851 circulation [of *Godey's Lady's Book*] reached 63,000, estimated to be twice that of any rival magazine, while by the eve of the Civil War that number was estimated to be over 150,000."

42. Joseph Michael Sommers, "*Godey's Lady's Book*: Sarah Hale and the Construction of Sentimental Nationalism," *College Literature* 37, no. 3 (2010): 43–61. Sommers argues that although Godey forbade political commentary, Hale used her role as editor to promote an antiwar stance during the antebellum era, partially through poems and essays that invoked the suffering and mourning of mothers during times of war.

43. Beverly Peterson, "Mrs. Hale on Mrs. Stowe and Slavery," *American Periodicals: A Journal of History, Criticism, and Bibliography* 8 (1998): 30–44; Marquita Walker, "Separate Spheres Collide: Slavery's Economic Influence on Domesticity in Sarah Josepha Hale's *Northwood* (1827 and 1852)," *Publications of the Missouri Philological Association* 25 (2000): 64–71; Kristina Marie Darling, "'Such Happiness Will Smile No More for Me': Domesticity, Women's Writing, and Sarah J. Hale's Editorial Career." *MP Journal* 2, no. 4 (2009): 14–29. Peterson, Walker, and Darling describe the various revisions Hale made before reissuing *Northwood*. All references for *Northwood* are to the 1852 edition.

44. Peterson, "Mrs. Hale on Mrs. Stowe and Slavery," 30. Peterson notes Hale's marked editorial silence on *Uncle Tom's Cabin*, the novel everyone was talking about. Although *Godey's Lady's Book* expressly avoided political issues, it contained reviews of popular literature and poetry, so Hale's decision to avoid reviewing or discussing a literary sensation makes its own statement. Ryan, "Errand into Africa," 582.

45. Sarah Josepha Hale, *Northwood; or, Life North and South: Showing the True Character of Both* (New York: H. Long & Brother, 1852), 401.

46. Hale, *Northwood*, 29.

47. Sarah Josepha Hale, *Manners, or, Happy Homes and Good Society All the Year Round* (Boston: J. E. Tilton, 1868; repr., New York: Arno Press, 1972), 315, emphasis in original.

48. Suzanne Gosset and Barbara Anne Bardes, "Women and Political Power In the Republic: Two Early American Novels," *Legacy* 2, no. 2 (1985): 19.

49. Hale, *Northwood*, 65.

50. Hale, *Northwood*, 132, 100.

51. Hale, *Northwood*, 156, 154.

52. Hale, *Northwood*, 85; Kaplan, "Manifest Domesticity," 589.

53. Frederick Douglass, "Narrative of the Life of Frederick Douglass, an American Slave, Written by Himself," in *The Norton Anthology of American Literature*, Shorter Eighth Edition, vol. 1, *Beginnings to 1865*, ed. Nina Baym and Robert S. Levine (New York: Norton, 2013), 956.

54. Douglass, "Narrative of the Life of Frederick Douglass," 999.

Conclusion

1. Pocock, *The Machiavellian Moment*, 466; Barbauld, *Sins of Government, Sins of the Nation*, 386.

2. Habermas, *The Inclusion of the Other*, 240, 252; Fraser, "Rethinking the Public Sphere"; Warner, *Publics and Counterpublics*; Berlant, *The Female Complaint*.

3. Ranciere, *Dissensus*, 51–52; Warner, *Publics and Counterpublics*, 114; Pocock, *The Machiavellian Moment*, 466.

4. Habermas, *The Inclusion of the Other*, 209–10; Pocock, *The Machiavellian Moment*, 464–75; Arendt, *The Human Condition*, 38–39; Douglass, "Narrative of the Life of Frederick Douglass," 960–61; Henry, *Liberalism and the Culture of Security*, 32.

5. Warner, *Publics and Counterpublics*, 11–16; "What We Believe," *Black Lives Matter*, https://blacklivesmatter.com/herstory/.

6. Jean-Francois Lyotard, *The Differend: Phrases in Dispute*, trans. George Van Den Abbeele (Minneapolis: University of Minnesota Press, 1988), 9.

7. Warner, *Publics and Counterpublics*, 26.

8. Robin Tolmach Lakoff, *The Language War* (Berkeley: University of California Press, 2000), 116–17.

9. Warner, *Publics and Counterpublics*, 12.

Aikin, John, and Anna Laetitia Barbauld. *Evenings at Home; or, the Juvenile Budget Opened: Consisting of a Variety of Miscellaneous Pieces . . .* Vol. 5. London: J. Johnson, 1796. Reprint, Ann Arbor, MI: Text Creation Partnership, 2009. ECCO-TCP.

Ammons, Elizabeth. "Heroines in Uncle Tom's Cabin." *American Literature* 49 (1977): 116–79. Reprint, *Critical Essays on Harriet Beecher Stowe*, edited by Elizabeth Ammons, 152–65. Boston: G. K. Hall, 1980.

Arendt, Hannah. *The Human Condition: A Study of the Central Dilemmas Facing Modern Man.* New York: Doubleday, 1959.

Aristotle. *Nichomachean Ethics.* Translated by W. D. Ross. Digireads.com, 2005.

Armstrong, Nancy, and Leonard Tennenhouse. *Novels in the Time of Democratic Writing: The American Example.* Philadelphia: University of Pennsylvania Press, 2018.

Ashworth, John. *"Agrarians" and "Aristocrats": Party Political Ideology in the United States, 1837–1846.* 1st ed. New York: Cambridge University Press, 1987.

Avallone, Charlene. "Catharine Sedgwick's White Nation-Making: Historical Fiction and *The Linwoods.*" *ESQ: A Journal of the American Renaissance* 55, no. 2 (2009): 97–133.

Axelrad, Allan M. "James Fenimore Cooper, American English, and the Signification of *Aristocracy* in a Republic." *Literature in the Early American Republic* 6 (2014): 137–70.

Backscheider, Paula R. *Eighteenth-Century Women Poets and Their Poetry: Inventing Agency, Inventing Genre.* Baltimore: Johns Hopkins University Press, 2005.

Bannett, Eve Tavor, and Susan Manning, eds. *Transatlantic Literary Studies, 1660–1830.* New York: Cambridge University Press, 2012.

Banning, Lance. "Some Second Thoughts on 'Virtue' and the Course of Revolutionary Thinking." In *Conceptual Change and the Constitution*, edited by Terence Ball and J. G. A. Pocock, 194–212. Lawrence: University Press of Kansas, 1988.

Barbauld, Anna Laetitia. "Civic Sermons to the People." London: Dundee, 1792. Google Books.

———. *Epistle to William Wilberforce, Esq. on the Rejection of the Bill for Abolishing the Slave Trade*. London: J. Johnson, 1791. http://www.brycchancarey.com/slavery/barbauld1.htm.

———. *Sins of Government, Sins of the Nation; or, a Discourse for the Fast, Appointed on April 19, 1793. By a Volunteer*. London: J. Johnson, 1793. Reprint, Ann Arbor: University of Michigan Library, 2007. ECCO-TCP.

Barker-Benfield, G. J. *The Culture of Sensibility: Sex and Society in Eighteenth-Century Britain*. Chicago: University of Chicago Press, 1992.

Bartolomeo, Joseph F. "No Place like Home: The Uses of America in 1790s British Fiction." *Yearbook of English Studies* 46 (2016): 242–58.

Baum, Rosalie Murphy. "*The Emigrants*: An American Utopia in Kentucky." *Journal of Kentucky Studies* 23 (2006): 154–65.

Baym, Nina. *American Women Writers and the Work of History, 1790–1860*. New Brunswick, NJ: Rutgers University Press, 1995.

Beard, James Franklin. "Cooper and the Revolutionary Mythos." *Early American Literature* 11, no. 1 (1976): 84–104.

Benhabib, Seyla. *Another Cosmopolitanism*. Oxford: Oxford University Press, 2006.

Berg, Maxine. *Luxury and Pleasure in Eighteenth-Century Britain*. New York: Oxford University Press, 2005.

Berlant, Lauren. *The Female Complaint: The Unfinished Business of Sentimentality in American Culture*. Durham, NC: Duke University Press, 2008.

———. *The Queen of America Goes to Washington City: Essays on Sex and Citizenship*. Durham, NC: Duke University Press, 1997.

Blaug, Richard. *Democracy, Real and Ideal: Discourse Ethics and Radical Politics*. Albany: State University of New York Press, 1999.

Bloom, Harold. *The Anxiety of Influence: A Theory of Poetry*. 2nd ed. New York: Oxford University Press, 1997.

Brown, Christopher Leslie. *Moral Capital: Foundations of British Abolitionism.* Chapel Hill: University of North Carolina Press, 2006.

Brown, Gillian. *Domestic Individualism: Imagining Self in Nineteenth-Century America.* Berkeley: University of California Press, 1990.

Budick, Emily Miller. *Fiction and Historical Consciousness: The American Romance Tradition.* New Haven: Yale University Press, 1989.

Burke, Edmund. *Reflections on the Revolution in France.* New York: Oxford University Press, 2009.

Burtt, Shelley. *Virtue Transformed: Political Argument in England, 1688–1740.* New York: Cambridge University Press, 1992.

Butler, Judith. *Undoing Gender.* New York: Routledge, 2004.

Card, Mary Birkett. *A Poem on the African Slave Trade: Addressed to Her Own Sex.* Dublin: J. Jones, 1792. http://www.brycchancarey.com/slavery/mbc1.htm.

Carrere, Marissa. "Theorizing Democratic Feelings, Disagreement, and the Temporal Child in Catharine Maria Sedgwick's *The Linwoods.*" *Legacy* 34, no. 1 (2017): 33–52.

Cayton, Andrew R. L. *Love in the Time of Revolution: Transatlantic Literary Radicalism and Historical Change, 1793–1818.* Chapel Hill: University of North Carolina Press, 2013.

Chard, Leslie F., II. "Joseph Johnson in the 1790s." *Wordsworth Circle* 33, no. 3 (2002): 95–100.

Clark, Robert. "Rewriting Revolution: Cooper's War of Independence." In *James Fenimore Cooper: New Critical Essays,* edited by Robert Clark, 187–205. Totowa, NJ: Barnes & Noble, 1985.

Colley, Linda. *Britons: Forging the Nation, 1701–1837.* New Haven: Yale University Press, 1992.

Cooper, Anthony Ashley, Earl of Shaftesbury. *Characteristicks of Men, Manners, Opinions, Times.* Vol. 2 (1737). Edited by Douglas Den Uyl. Indianapolis: Liberty Fund, 2001. Online Library of Liberty.

Cooper, James Fenimore. *The American Democrat.* Cooperstown, NY: Elihu Phinney, 1838. Reprint, New York: Barnes & Noble, 2004.

———. *Notions of the Americans: Picked Up by a Travelling Bachelor.* Vol. 2. Philadelphia: Carey, Lea, & Blanchard, 1828. Nabu Public Domain Reprints. https://archive.org/stream/cihm_50256?ref=ol#mode/2up.

———. *The Spy: A Tale of the Neutral Ground*. New York: Wiley, 1821. Reprint, New York: Penguin, 1997.

Copeland, David A. *The Antebellum Era: Primary Documents on Events from 1820 to 1860*. Westport, CT: Greenwood, 2003.

Crawford, Hugh. "Cooper's Spy and the Theater of Honor." *American Literature* 63, no. 3 (1991): 405–19.

Daly, Robert. "Reading Sedgwick Now: Empathy and Ethics in Early America." *Literature in the Early American Republic* 2 (2010): 131–52.

Damon-Bach, Lucinda L., and Victoria Clements, eds. *Catharine Maria Sedgwick: Critical Perspectives*. Boston: Northeastern University Press, 2003.

Darling, Kristina Marie. "'Such Happiness Will Smile No More for Me': Domesticity, Women's Writing, and Sarah J. Hale's Editorial Career." *MP Journal* 2, no. 4 (2009): 14–29.

Davidson, Cathy N., ed. *No More Separate Spheres! A Next Wave American Studies Reader*. Durham, NC: Duke University Press, 2002.

"Debate in the Commons on the King's Proclamation against Seditious Writings." In *The Parliamentary History of England from the Earliest Period to the Year 1803*. Vol. 29. London: T. C. Hansard, 1817: 1476–90. Google Books.

DeLucia, JoEllen. *A Feminine Enlightenment: British Women Writers and the Philosophy of Progress, 1759–1820*. Edinburgh: Edinburgh University Press, 2015.

Dillon, Elizabeth Maddock. *The Gender of Freedom: Fictions of Liberalism and the Literary Public Sphere*. Stanford, CA: Stanford University Press, 2004.

Doolen, Andy. "Blood, Republicanism, and the Return of George Washington: A Response to Shirley Samuels." *American Literary History* 20, no. 1/2 (2008): 76–82.

Douglas, Ann. *The Feminization of American Culture*. 1st ed. New York: Knopf, 1977.

Douglass, Frederick. "Narrative of the Life of Frederick Douglass, an American Slave, Written by Himself." In *The Norton Anthology of American Literature*, Shorter Eighth Edition, vol. 1, *Beginnings to 1865*, edited by Nina Baym and Robert S. Levine, 938–1000. New York: Norton, 2013.

Ellis, Markman. *The Politics of Sensibility: Race, Gender, and Commerce in the Sentimental Novel*. New York: Cambridge University Press, 1996.

Emerson, Amanda. "History, Memory, and the Echoes of Equivalence in Catharine Maria Sedgwick's *Hope Leslie*." *Legacy* 24, no. 1 (2007): 24–49.

Emerson, Oliver Farrar. "Notes on Gilbert Imlay, Early American Writer." *PMLA: Publications of the Modern Language Association of America* 39, no. 2 (1924): 406–39.

Emerson, Ralph Waldo. "The American Scholar." In *The Norton Anthology of American Literature*, Shorter Eighth Edition, vol. 1, *Beginnings to 1865*, edited by Nina Baym and Robert S. Levine, 536–49. New York: Norton, 2013.

Eustace, Nicole. *Passion Is the Gale: Emotion, Power, and the Coming of the American Revolution*. Chapel Hill: University of North Carolina Press, 2008.

Fagan, Jean Yellin. "Doing It Herself: *Uncle Tom's Cabin* and Woman's Role in the Slavery Crisis." In *New Essays on Uncle Tom's Cabin*, edited by Eric J. Sundquist, 81–106. Cambridge: Cambridge University Press, 1986.

Falconar, Maria, and Harriet Falconar. *Poems on Slavery*. London: Egertons, Murray, & Johnson, 1788. http://www.brycchancarey.com/slavery/falconar.htm.

Ferguson, Moira. *Subject to Others: British Women Writers and Colonial Slavery, 1670–1834*. New York: Routledge, 1992.

Fiedler, Leslie A. *Love and Death in the American Novel*. New York: Criterion, 1960.

Finley, Ruth E. *The Lady of* Godey's: *Sarah Josepha Hale*. New York: Arno, 1974.

Fitzgibbons, Athol. *Adam Smith's System of Liberty, Wealth, and Virtue: The Moral and Political Foundations of* The Wealth of Nations. New York: Clarendon Press, 1995.

Fraser, Nancy. "Rethinking the Public Sphere: A Contribution to the Critique of Actually Existing Democracy." *Social Text* 25/26 (1990): 56–80.

Funchion, John. "Reading Less Littorally: Kentucky and the Translocal Imagination in the Atlantic World." *Early American Literature* 48, no. 1 (2013): 61–91. https://doi.org/10.1353/eal.2013.0015.

Gallagher, Noelle. "The Bagging Factory and the Breakfast Factory: Industrial

Labor and Sentimentality in Harriet Beecher Stowe's *Uncle Tom's Cabin*." *Nineteenth-Century Contexts* 27, no. 2 (2005): 167–87.

Ginzberg, Lori D. "Virtue and Violence: Female Ultraists and the Politics of Non-Resistance." *Quaker History* 84, no. 1 (1995): 17–25.

Gosset, Suzanne, and Barbara Anne Bardes. "Women and Political Power in the Early Republic: Two Early American Novels." *Legacy* 2, no. 2 (1985): 13–30.

Gosset, Thomas F. Uncle Tom's Cabin *and American Culture*. Dallas: Southern Methodist University Press, 1985.

Gould, Philip. *Covenant and Republic: Historical Romance and the Politics of Puritanism*. New York: Cambridge University Press, 1996.

Greenberg, Hope. "*Godey's Lady's Book*: Publication History." University of Vermont. http://www.uvm.edu/~hag/godey/glbpub.html.

Habermas, Jürgen. *The Inclusion of the Other: Studies in Political Theory*. Edited by Ciaran Cronin and Pablo De Greiff. Cambridge: MIT Press, 1998.

———. *The Structural Transformation of the Public Sphere: An Inquiry into a Category of Bourgeois Society*. Translated by Thomas Burger with the assistance of Frederick Lawrence. Cambridge: MIT Press, 1991.

Hada, Kenneth. "The Kentucky Model: Economics, Individualism, and Domesticity in *Uncle Tom's Cabin*." *Papers on Language and Literature: A Journal for Scholars and Critics of Language and Literature* 35, no. 2 (1999): 167–86.

Hale, Sarah Josepha. *Liberia; or, Mr. Peyton's Experiments*. New York: Harper & Brothers, 1853. Reprint, Upper Saddle River, NJ: Gregg, 1968.

———. *Manners; or, Happy Homes and Good Society All the Year Round*. Boston: J. E. Tilton, 1868. Reprint, New York: Arno Press, 1972.

———. *Northwood; or, Life North and South: Showing the True Character of Both*. New York: H. Long & Brother, 1852. Google Books.

Harrington, Dana. "Gender, Commerce, and the Transformation of Virtue in Eighteenth-Century Britain." *Rhetoric Society Quarterly* 31, no. 3 (2001): 33–52.

Harris, Christopher. *Public Lives, Private Virtues: Images of American Revolutionary War Heroes, 1782–1832*. New York: Garland, 2000.

Harris, Susan K. "The Limits of Authority: Catharine Maria Sedgwick and the Politics of Resistance." In *Catharine Maria Sedgwick: Critical*

Perspectives, edited by Lucinda L. Damon-Bach and Victoria Clements. Boston: Northeastern University Press, 2003, 272–85.

Hart, Monica Smith. "Protest and Performance: Ann Yearsley's Poems on Several Occasions." In *The Working-Class Intellectual in Eighteenth- and Nineteenth-Century Britain*, 49–66. Surrey, Eng.: Ashgate, 2009.

Henry, Katherine. *Liberalism and the Culture of Security: The Nineteenth-Century Rhetoric of Reform*. Tuscaloosa: University of Alabama Press, 2011.

"Herstory." *Black Lives Matter*. http://blacklivesmatter.com/about/herstory/.

Hovet, Ted, Jr. "Harriet Martineau's Exceptional American Narratives: Harriet Beecher Stowe, John Brown, and the 'Redemption of Your National Soul.'" *American Studies* 48, no. 1 (2007): 63–76.

Hume, David. "Of Commerce." *Essays, Moral, Political, and Literary*. Edited by Eugene F. Miller. London: Millar, Kincaid, & Donaldson, 1889. Reprint, Indianapolis: Liberty Fund, 1987. Online Library of Liberty.

———. "Of National Characters." *Essays, Moral, Political, and Literary*. Edited by Eugene F. Miller. London: Millar, Kincaid, & Donaldson, 1889. Reprint, Indianapolis: Liberty Fund, 1987. Online Library of Liberty.

———. "Of Refinement in the Arts." *Essays, Moral, Political, and Literary*. Edited by Eugene F. Miller. London: Millar, Kincaid, & Donaldson, 1889. Reprint, Indianapolis: Liberty Fund, 1987. Online Library of Liberty.

Ickstadt, Heinz. "Instructing the American Democrat: Cooper and the Concept of Popular Fiction in Jacksonian America." In *James Fenimore Cooper: New Critical Essays*, edited by Robert Clark, 15–37. Harrisonburg, VA: Vision Publishers, 1985.

Imlay, Gilbert. *The Emigrants*. 1793. Reprint, New York: Penguin, 1998.

———. *A Topographical Description of the Western Territory of North America; Containing a Succinct Account of Its Soil, Climate, Natural History, Population, Agriculture, Manners and Customs*. 3rd ed. London: J. Debrett, 1797. Reprint, New York: A. M. Kelly, 1969.

Ingrassia, Catherine. "Contesting 'Home' in Eighteenth-Century Women's Verse." In *Home and Nation in British Literature from the English to the French Revolutions*, edited by A. D. Cousins and Geoffrey Payne, 154–68. New York: Cambridge University Press, 2015.

Jennings, Judith. *The Business of Abolishing the British Slave Trade*. London: Routledge, 1997.

Kammen, Michael. *A Season of Youth: The American Revolution and the Historical Imagination*. New York: Knopf, 1978.

Kane, John. *The Politics of Moral Capital*. New York: Cambridge University Press, 2001.

Kant, Immanuel. "An Answer to the Question: 'What Is Enlightenment?'" In *The Idea of the Public Sphere: A Reader*, edited by Jostein Gripsrud, Hallvard Moe, Anders Mollander, Graham Murdock, 3–8. New York: Rowan & Littlefield, 2010.

Kaplan, Amy. *The Anarchy of Empire in the Making of U.S. Culture*. Cambridge, MA: Harvard University Press, 2002.

———. "Manifest Domesticity." *American Literature: A Journal of Literary History, Criticism, and Bibliography* 70, no. 3 (1998): 581–606.

Karafilis, Maria. "Catharine Maria Sedgwick's *Hope Leslie*: The Crisis between Ethical Political Action and US Literary Nationalism in the New Republic." *American Transcendental Quarterly* 12, no. 4 (1998): 327–44.

———. Introduction to *The Linwoods; or, "Sixty Years Since" in America*, xi–xxxv. Hanover, NH: University Press of New England, 2002.

Karcher, Carolyn L. "Catharine Maria Sedgwick in Literary History." In *Catharine Maria Sedgwick: Critical Perspectives*, edited by Lucinda L. Damon-Bach and Victoria Clements, 5–16. Boston: Northeastern University Press, 2003.

Kaye, F. B. Introduction to *The Fable of the Bees: or, Private Vices, Publick Benefits* (1732 edition), xvii–cxlv. Oxford: Clarendon Press, 1924.

Kennedy, J. Gerald. *Strange Nation: Literary Nationalism and Cultural Conflict in the Age of Poe*. Oxford: Oxford University Press, 2016.

Kerber, Linda. "The Republican Mother: Women and the Enlightenment—An American Perspective." *American Quarterly* 28, no. 2 (1976): 187–205.

———. *Women of the Republic: Intellect and Ideology in Revolutionary America*. Chapel Hill: University of North Carolina Press, 1980.

Kilgore, John Mac. "John Lithgow's Real Utopia and the Anticapitalist Romance of the Early Republic." *Early American Literature* 54, no. 1 (2019): 97–133.

Kligerman, Jack. "Notes on Cooper's Debt to John Jay." *American Literature: A Journal of Literary History, Criticism, and Bibliography* 41, no. 3 (November 1969): 415–19.

Knott, Sarah. *Sensibility and the American Revolution.* Chapel Hill: University of North Carolina Press, 2009.

Lakoff, Robin Tolmach. *The Language War.* Berkeley: University of California Press, 2000.

Locke, John. *Two Treatises on Government and a Letter Concerning Toleration.* London: Churchill, 1689–90. Reprint, edited by Ian Shapiro. New Haven: Yale University Press, 2003.

Logan, Deborah Anna. *The Hour and the Woman: Harriet Martineau's "Somewhat Remarkable" Life.* DeKalb: Northern Illinois University Press, 2002.

———. "'My Dearly-Beloved Americans': Harriet Martineau's Transatlantic Abolitionism." In *Nineteenth-Century British Travelers in the New World*, edited by Christine DeVine, 203–20. Burlington, VT: Ashgate Press, 2013.

Lootens, Tricia A. *The Political Poetess: Victorian Femininity, Race, and the Legacy of Separate Spheres.* Princeton: Princeton University Press, 2017.

Lyotard, Jean-Francois. *The Differend: Phrases in Dispute.* Translated by Georges Van Den Abbeele. Minneapolis: University of Minnesota Press, 1988.

Major, Emma. "Ithuriel's Spear: Barbauld, Sermons, and Citizens, 1789–93." *Journal for Eighteenth-Century Studies* 41, no. 2 (2018): 257–72.

Mallipeddi, Ramesh. *Spectacular Suffering: Witnessing Slavery in the Eighteenth-Century British Atlantic.* Charlottesville: University of Virginia Press, 2016.

Mandeville, Bernard. *The Fable of the Bees: or, Private Vices, Publick Benefits (1732 edition). With a Commentary Critical, Historical, and Explanatory by F. B. Kaye*, vol. 1. Oxford: Clarendon Press, 1924.

Manning, Susan, and Andrew Taylor, eds. *Transatlantic Literary Studies: A Reader.* Baltimore: Johns Hopkins University Press, 2007.

Martineau, Harriet. "Demerara." In *Illustrations of Political Economy*, 3rd ed. London: Charles Fox, 1832. Online Library of Liberty.

———. *Harriet Martineau's Autobiography.* Boston: James R. Osgood, 1877. Reprint, London: Virago, 1983.

———. *How to Observe Morals and Manners*. London: Charles Knight, 1838. Reprint, Charleston, SC: BiblioLife, 2009.

———. "The Martyr Age of the United States." *Westminster Review* (December 1838). Reprint, New York: Arno Press, 1969.

———. *Retrospect of Western Travel*. London: Saunders & Otley, 1838. Reprint, New York: Greenwood, 1969.

———. *Society in America*. New York: Saunders & Otley, 1837. Reprint, New York: Anchor Books, 1962.

———. *Writings on Slavery and the American Civil War*. Edited by Deborah Logan. DeKalb: Northern Illinois University Press, 2002.

Mazzeo, Tilar J. "The Impossibility of Being Anglo-American: The Rhetoric of Emigration and Transatlanticism in British Romantic Culture, 1791–1833." *European Romantic Review* 16, no. 1 (2005): 59–78.

McDowell, Tremaine. "The Identity of Harvey Birch." *American Literature: A Journal of Literary History, Criticism, and Bibliography* 2, no. 2 (May 1930): 111–20.

McWilliams, John P., Jr. "Cooper and the Conservative Democrat." *American Quarterly* 22 (1970): 665–77.

———. *Political Justice in a Republic: James Fenimore Cooper's America*. Berkeley: University of California Press, 1972.

Mellor, Anne K. "The Female Poet and the Poetess: Two Traditions of British Women's Poetry, 1780–1830." *Studies in Romanticism* 36, no. 2 (1997): 261–76.

———. *Mothers of the Nation: Women's Political Writing in England, 1780–1830*. Bloomington: Indiana University Press, 2000.

Merish, Lori. *Sentimental Materialism: Gender, Commodity Culture, and Nineteenth-Century American Literature*. Durham, NC: Duke University Press, 2000.

Miller, Mark J. *Cast Down: Abjection in America, 1700–1850*. Philadelphia: University of Pennsylvania Press, 2016.

More, Hannah. *Slavery: A Poem*. London: T. Cadell, 1788. http://www.brycchancarey.com/slavery/morepoems.htm.

"More Than 12M 'Me Too' Facebook Posts, Comments, Reactions in 24 Hours." CBS News online, October 17, 2017.

Morgan, Kenneth. *Slavery, Atlantic Trade, and the British Economy, 1660–1800.* New York: Cambridge University Press, 2000.

Morse, David. *The Age of Virtue: British Culture from the Restoration to Romanticism.* New York: Palgrave, 2000.

Mullan, John. *Sentiment and Sociability: The Language of Feeling in the Eighteenth Century.* New York: Oxford University Press, 1988.

Muller, Jerry Z. *The Mind and the Market: Capitalism in Modern European Thought.* New York: Knopf, 2002.

O'Brien, Karen. *Women and Enlightenment in Eighteenth-Century Britain.* New York: Cambridge University Press, 2009.

Opfermann, Susanne. "Lydia Maria Child, James Fenimore Cooper, and Catharine Maria Sedgwick: A Dialogue on Race, Culture, and Gender." In *Soft Canons: American Women Writers and Masculine Tradition,* edited by Karen L. Kilcup, 27–47. Iowa City: University of Iowa Press, 1999.

Peterson, Beverly. "Mrs. Hale on Mrs. Stowe and Slavery." *American Periodicals: A Journal of History, Criticism, and Bibliography* 8 (1998): 30–44.

Phillips, Anne. *Engendering Democracy.* University Park: Pennsylvania State University Press, 1991.

Pichanick, Valerie Kossew. "An Abominable Submission: Harriet Martineau's Views of the Role and Place of Women." *Women's Studies: An Interdisciplinary Journal* 5 (1977): 13–32.

Piep, Karsten H. "Separatist Nationalism in Gilbert Imlay's *The Emigrants.*" *CLCWeb: Comparative Literature and Culture* 6, no. 4 (2004): 1–9. https://doi.org/10.7771/1481-4374.1247.

Pocock, J. G. A. *The Machiavellian Moment: Florentine Political Thought and the Atlantic Republican Tradition.* Princeton: Princeton University Press, 1975.

Pohl, Nicole, and Brenda Tooley, eds. *Gender and Utopia in the Eighteenth Century: Essays in English and French Utopian Writing.* Burlington, VT: Ashgate, 2007.

Raifman, Julia, Ellen Moscoe, S. Bryn Austin, and Margaret McConnell. "Difference-in-Differences Analysis of the Association between State Same-Sex Marriage Policies and Adolescent Suicide Attempts." *JAMA Pediatrics* 171, no. 4 (2017): 350–56.

Ranciere, Jacques. *Dissensus: On Politics and Aesthetics*. Translated by Steven Corcoran. New York: Continuum, 2010.

Rawls, John. *Political Liberalism*. Expanded ed. New York: Columbia University Press, 2005.

Rendall, Jane. "Virtue and Commerce: Women in the Making of Adam Smith's Political Economy." In *Women in Western Political Philosophy: Kant to Nietzsche*, edited by Ellen Kennedy and Susan Mendus, 44–77. New York: St. Martin's Press, 1987.

Reynolds, David S. *Mightier Than the Sword*: Uncle Tom's Cabin *and the Battle for America*. 1st ed. New York: W. W. Norton, 2011.

Robin, Corey. *The Reactionary Mind: Conservatism from Edmund Burke to Sarah Palin*. Oxford: Oxford University Press, 2013.

Ryan, Susan M. "Errand into Africa: Colonization and Nation Building in Sarah J. Hale's *Liberia*." *New England Quarterly* 68, no. 4 (1995): 558–83.

Salam, Maya. "Brock Turner Is Appealing His Sexual Assault Conviction." *New York Times* online, December 2, 2017.

Sambrook, James. *The Eighteenth Century: The Intellectual and Cultural Context of English Literature, 1700–1789*. New York: Longman, 1986.

Samuels, Shirley K. *The Culture of Sentiment: Race, Gender, and Sentimentality in Nineteenth-Century America*. New York: Oxford University Press, 1992.

———. *Reading the American Novel, 1780–1865*. Malden, MA: Wiley-Blackwell, 2012.

———. *Romances of the Republic: Women, the Family, and Violence in the Literature of the Early American Nation*. New York: Oxford University Press, 1996.

———. "Women, Blood, and Contract." *American Literary History* 20, 1–2 (2008): 57–75.

Santiago, Cassandra, and Doug Criss. "An Activist, a Little Girl and the Heartbreaking Origin of 'Me Too.'" CNN online, October 17, 2017.

Schlesinger, Arthur, Jr. *The Age of Jackson*. Boston: Little, Brown, 1945.

Scott, Joan Wallach. *Gender and the Politics of History*. New York: Columbia University Press, 1988

Sedgwick, Catharine Maria. *Hope Leslie; or, Early Times in Massachusetts*. 1827. Reprint, edited by Maria Karafilis. New York: Penguin, 1998.

———. *The Linwoods; or, "Sixty Years Since" in America*. New York: Harper & Brothers, 1835. Reprint, Hanover, NH: University Press of New England, 2002.

———. *The New England Tale*. New York: E. Bliss and E. White, 1822. Reprint, New York: Penguin, 2003.

———. *The Poor Rich Man, and the Rich Poor Man*. New York: Harper & Brothers, 1836. Reprint, Farmington Hills, MI: Gale, Sabin Americana, 2012.

———. *The Power of Her Sympathy: The Autobiography and Journal of Catharine Maria Sedgwick*. Edited by Mary Kelley. Boston: Massachusetts Historical Society, 1993.

Seelye, John. "The Jacobin Mode in Early American Fiction: Gilbert Imlay's *The Emigrants*." *Early American Literature* 22, no. 2 (1987): 204–12.

Shapiro, Joe. *The Illiberal Imagination: Class and the Rise of the U.S. Novel*. Charlottesville: University of Virginia Press, 2017.

Shields, Juliet. "Genuine Sentiments and Gendered Liberties: Migration and Marriage in Gilbert Imlay's *The Emigrants*." In *Atlantic Worlds in the Long Eighteenth Century: Seduction and Sentiment*, edited by Toni Bowers and Tita Chico, 33–47. New York: Palgrave Macmillan, 2012.

———. *Nation and Migration: The Making of British Atlantic Literature, 1765–1835*. Oxford: Oxford University Press, 2016.

Shovlin, John. *The Political Economy of Virtue: Luxury, Patriotism, and the Origins of the French Revolution*. Ithaca, NY: Cornell University Press, 2006.

Skinner, Gillian. *Sensibility and Economics in the Novel, 1740–1800: The Price of a Tear*. New York: St. Martin's, 1999.

Smith, Adam. *An Inquiry into the Nature and Causes of the Wealth of Nations*. London: W. Strahan & T. Cadell, 1776. Reprint, edited by Jim Manis. Hazelton: Pennsylvania State University, 2005. http://www.rrojasdatabank.info/adamsmith/wealthp1.pdf.

———. *The Theory of Moral Sentiments*. London: A. Millar, A. Kincaid, & J. Bell, 1759. Reprint, New York: Classic House Books, 2009.

Sommers, Joseph Michael. "*Godey's Lady's Book*: Sarah Hale and the Construction of Sentimental Nationalism." *College Literature* 37, no. 3 (2010): 43–61.

Spelman, Elizabeth. *Fruits of Sorrow: Framing Our Attention to Suffering*. Boston: Beacon Press, 1998.

St. Armond, Barton Levi. "Harvey Birch as the Wandering Jew: Literary Calvinism in James Fenimore Cooper's *The Spy*." *American Literature* 50, no. 3 (Nov. 1978): 348–68.

Stein, Jordan Alexander. "'A Christian Nation Calls for Its Wandering Children': Life, Liberty, Liberia." *American Literary History* 19, no. 4 (2007): 849–73.

Stevens, Laura M. "Transatlanticism Now." *American Literary History* 16, no. 1 (2004): 93–102.

St. John de Crèvecoeur, Hector J. *Letters from an American Farmer*. London: Davies & Davis, 1782. Reprint, New York: J. M. Dent & Sons, 1912.

Stowe, Harriet Beecher. *Uncle Tom's Cabin*. Boston: John P. Jewett, 1852. Reprint, New York: Oxford World Classics, 1998.

Sundquist, Eric J. *Empire and Slavery in American Literature, 1820–1865*. Jackson: University Press of Mississippi, 2006.

Sussman, Charlotte. *Consuming Anxieties: Consumer Protest, Gender, and British Slavery, 1713–1833*. Stanford, CA: Stanford University Press, 2000.

Swaminathan, Srividhya, and Adam R. Beach, eds. *Invoking Slavery in the Eighteenth-Century British Imagination*. Surrey, Eng.: Ashgate Press, 2013.

Taketani, Etsuko. "Postcolonial Liberia: Sarah Josepha Hale's Africa." *American Literary History* 14, no. 3 (2002): 479–504.

Thoreau, Henry David. *Walden, Civil Disobedience, and Other Writings*. Boston: Ticknor & Fields, 1854. Reprint, New York: Norton, 2008.

Tocqueville, Alexis de. *Democracy in America and Two Essays on America*. London: Saunders & Otley, 1835–40. Reprint, edited by Isaac Kramnick, New York: Penguin, 2003.

Todd, Janet. *Death and the Maidens: Fanny Wollstonecraft and the Shelley Circle*. Berkeley, CA: Counterpoint, 2007.

Tompkins, Jane P. *Sensational Designs: The Cultural Work of American Fiction, 1790–1860*. New York: Oxford University Press, 1985.

Trethewey, Rachel. "Lady Defender of the Revolution: Barbauld among the British Radicals." In *Anna Letitia Barbauld: New Perspectives*, edited by William McCarthy and Olivia Murphy, 151–72. Lanham, MD: Bucknell University Press, 2014.

VanDette, Emily. "'It Should Be a Family Thing': Family, Nation, and Republicanism in Catharine Maria Sedgwick's *A New England Tale* and *The Linwoods*." *ATQ: 19th Century American Literature and Culture* 19, no. 1 (2005): 51–74.

Verhoeven, Wil M. *Americomania and the French Revolution Debate in Britain, 1789–1802*. New York: Cambridge University Press, 2013.

———. "Gilbert Imlay and the Triangular Trade." *William and Mary Quarterly*, 3rd ser., 63, no. 4 (2006): 827–42.

———. *Gilbert Imlay: Citizen of the World*. London: Pickering & Chatto, 2008.

———. "'New Philosophers' in the Backwoods: Romantic Primitivism in the 1790s' Novel." *Wordsworth Circle* 32, no. 3 (2001): 130–33.

Verhoeven, Wil M., and Amanda Gilroy. Introduction to *The Emigrants*. New York: Penguin, 1998.

Verhoeven, Wil M., Claudia L. Johnson, Philip Cox, Amanda Gilroy, and Robert Miles, editors. *Anti-Jacobin Novels*, vols. 1–5. New York: Routledge, 2017.

Walker, Marquita. "Separate Spheres Collide: Slavery's Economic Influence on Domesticity in Sarah Josepha Hale's *Northwood* (1827 and 1852)." *Publications of the Missouri Philological Association* 25 (2000): 64–71.

Waples, Dorothy. *The Whig Myth of James Fenimore Cooper*. Hamden, CT: Archon, 1968.

Warner, Michael. *Publics and Counterpublics*. New York: Zone Books, 2002.

Webb, R. K. *Harriet Martineau: A Radical Victorian*. New York: Columbia University Press, 1960.

Weyler, Karen E. *Empowering Words: Outsiders and Authorship in Early America*. Athens: University of Georgia Press, 2013.

"What We Believe." Black Lives Matter. https://blacklivesmatter.com/about/what-we-believe/.

Wilson, Brett D. "Hannah More's Slavery and James Thomson's Liberty: Fond Links, Mad Liberty, and Unfeeling Bondage." In *Invoking Slavery in the Eighteenth-Century British Imagination*, edited by Srividhya Swaminathan and Adam R. Beach, 93–114. Surrey, Eng.: Ashgate Press, 2013.

Wood, Gordon S. *The Creation of the American Republic, 1776–1787*. Chapel Hill: University of North Carolina Press, 1969.

Wooden, Shannon R. "Two Generations of Women's Abolitionist Poetry: Nation to Transnation, Revolution to Metaphor." In *Revolutions and Watersheds: Transatlantic Dialogues, 1775–1815*, 145–67. Amsterdam: Rodopi, 1999.

Yearsley, Ann. *A Poem on the Inhumanity of the Slave Trade*. London: G. G. J. & J. Robinson, 1788. http://www.brycchancarey.com/slavery/yearsley1 .htm.

Young, Alfred E. *The Shoemaker and the Tea Party: Memory and American Revolution*. Boston: Beacon Press, 1999.

Zacharek, Stephanie, Eliana Dockterman, and Haley Sweetland Edwards. "*Time* Person of the Year 2017: The Silence Breakers." Time.com.

Index